MW01165706

With Rifle and Petticoat

With Rifle and Petticoat

Women as Big Game Hunters, 1880–1940

KENNETH P. CZECH

THE DERRYDALE PRESS
Lanham and New York

THE DERRYDALE PRESS

Published in the United States of America
by The Derrydale Press
A Member of the Rowman & Littlefield Publishing Group
4720 Boston Way, Lanham, Maryland 20706

Distributed by NATIONAL BOOK NETWORK, INC.

Copyright © 2002 The Derrydale Press

Library of Congress Cataloging-in-Publication Data
Czech, Kenneth P.
With rifle and petticoat : women as big game hunters / Ken Czech.
p. cm
Includes bibliographical references.
ISBN 1-58667-082-4 (cloth : alk. paper)
1. Women hunters—History. 2. Big game hunting—History. I. Title.
SK21 .C94 2002
799.2'6'082—dc21 2002004482

All rights reserved. No part of this publication may be reproduced, stored in a retrieval system, or transmitted in any form or by any means, electronic, mechanical, photocopying, recording, or otherwise, without the prior permission of the publisher.

∞™ The paper used in this publication meets the minimum requirements of American National Standard for Information Sciences—Permanence of Paper for Printed Library Materials, ANSI/NISO Z39.48–1992.
Manufactured in the United States of America.

Contents

Acknowledgments

While compiling an annotated bibliography of books related to hunting big game in Africa a few years ago, I was struck that several books were written by women. An examination of the literature of hunting in Asia and North America revealed a handful of women hunters in those regions as well. When taken in total, women big game hunters combined to produce a significant body of writing describing their adventures. The difficulty in researching a book detailing their experiences was in locating the books they had written, especially since few ever went beyond their initial printing run, or they were privately printed in very small numbers.

In helping locate sources of information, I would like to thank Joan O'Driscoll of the Inter-Library Loan desk at St. Cloud State University for patiently plying through my requests and tracking down these elusive volumes. I would also like to thank the staff at the Houston County Historical Society in Winona, Minnesota for their aid in accessing documents on Grace King.

A number of antiquarian book dealers and collectors generously lent me rare books from their collections including Carol Lueder of Fair Chase Inc.; David Foley of David Foley Sporting Books; and Arnold

"Jake" Johnson. Norden Van Horne also supplied a list of books by sportswomen he has collected. Both Troy Bassett and Laura Franey graciously supplied drafts of papers on women hunters and explorers they presented at scholarly conferences. Theodore J. Holsten, Jr., a knowledgeable bookseller and editor, provided valuable comments on my manuscript.

My chapter on Agnes Herbert was originally presented at the Northern Great Plains History Conference in St. Cloud, Minnesota in October, 1999.

I would like to thank Kathleen Klehr and Ann Leger-Anderson for their comments on that paper. I would like to especially thank Mathew "Duke" Biscotti for his interest in my work, reading the manuscript and directing me toward The Derrydale Press. Additional thanks go to Stephen Driver, associate editor at Derrydale.

Foreword

They talk about "a woman's sphere"
As though it has a limit;
(Yet) there's not a spot on sea or shore,
In sanctum, office, shop or store,
Without a woman in it.

Author Unknown, written circa 1905

I grew up in the 1950s, graduated from college in the mid-1960s, and started my own business in the early 1970s. Those were the days when one often heard questions like "Is she going, too?" and "Will there be any extra women?" (I still defy anyone to explain that phrase.) In fact, thanks to the fact that our then state governor defined women as a legal minority in California, I was able to get a 3 percent simple-interest business loan.

Not long afterward I became the first woman to be accepted as an official measurer by the Boone & Crockett Club. With glee I carefully folded my official notification and dashed off a letter to my then British co-publisher of big game hunting books. Soon his response came in the mail.

"Why should I congratulate you when all this means is that another bastion of male chauvinism has gone to hell in America!" Even today my response is not printable. He is no longer my publishing partner.

The incident, however, aroused my curiosity. Here I was, dealing in antiquarian and new big game hunting books, most of which were authored by men. Most? Ninety-nine percent. Had not women been hunting for a long time? Were they not often- sometimes- the equals of their male counterparts? Did not many professional hunters in Africa and guides in North America comment on how well women performed in the field? Why, then, were there not more women in the big game hunting fraternity (and it was a fraternity)? And why were there not more books authored by women?

The answer was obvious. For many years, women filled the traditional roles of their day. Daughter, sister, wife, mother. Later perhaps they took jobs that fit the "feminine" image—secretary, teacher, nurse, etc. Therefore, the first women who ventured into Africa did so often in the dual role of explorer/companion to their husband or along with a missionary. The husbands authored the books, and the women's roles were sometimes noted, though usually as afterthoughts.

Some women found they enjoyed the sport, but becoming accepted as a big game huntress implied pioneering a long road in the 1800s. And even if a woman did achieve some measure of success in her travel and exploration or big game hunting endeavors, finding a publisher in this male-dominated sport was difficult indeed. Furthermore, it was the men who purchased the books. (By the way, this is true even today.) Rowland Ward noted in his autobiography, with some surprise, that Agnes Herbert took better specimens of tur in the Caucasus than most men. It was an age-old concept: If a man got a good trophy, it was because of skill; if a woman bagged a good trophy, it was due to Lady Luck.

As time went on, more and more women ventured into the hunting field. Museums actively started to collect natural-history specimens, so more European hunters were sent to collect them. Wives often accompanied their husbands. In the case of some, like Vivienne de Watteville, they carried on after the male leader passed away. In other cases, women like Gabrielle Vassal found that their doctor husbands were more interested in treating natives and were content to let them provide food for the table.

As Europeans raced to colonize Africa, many men were sent to the Dark Continent (and elsewhere), and women accompanied them. When wars raged, men went to fight while the women were left to protect the farms and homesteads with their rifles. The legendary American pioneer Charles Cottar believed that teaching his daughters to shoot and hunt was one of the most important facets of their upbringing.

So it was probably during the period between the two world wars that women started to be accepted as big game hunters in their own right, when we started seeing more women afield and more women with the courage to record their exploits for the reading public. However, publishers remained cautious, and print runs were not large. It was sort of a chicken-and-egg situation: Publishers didn't print lots of copies of books authored by women so they didn't have to spend a big part of their ad budgets on them. When they sold out, they were not reprinted. As a result, today many of the books authored by women are far less common than those authored by their male counterparts.

Then several extremely outgoing women burst onto the scene. Karen Blixen (Isak Dinesen) and Osa Johnson certainly achieved enormous popularity and publicity, while the Akeley women proved themselves competent in the field. Martin and Osa Johnson not only wrote books but also took advantage of that other medium so popular in America, the motion picture. Thousands of men and women saw their movies as well as read their books. Little by little, it was accepted to bring women on safari. An interesting side note: The noted Sudan game warden, H. C. Brocklehurst was in fact divorced from his wife after the turn of the last century because he took women on safari. In Kenyan law, that was an acceptable reason for divorce. Perhaps it's still a valid reason today. (The more things change)

As a result of this somewhat changed attitude, we saw more women hunting internationally, hunting dangerous game, and recording their exploits and having them published. The reading public was still male-dominated and not large. However, women became accepted as huntresses and authors. Perhaps I am prejudiced, but if you did not know the gender of the authors, these works stand up to those books written by men.

Amazingly, this book by Ken Czech is the first to deal specifically with women as big game hunters and authors of big game hunting books. As you will see, their accomplishments in the hunting field have been substantial, and their writing is "darn good."

I've been hunting for almost thirty years and have been authoring and publishing for almost as many years (perhaps this should not be admitted). I hope this is the first in a series of books on the subject of women in the hunting field. Because one thing is sure: If you ask the question "Is she going, too?" Today, the answer is going to be "Yes."

Ellen Enzler-Herring
Agoura, California

ONE

Dianas at the Hunt: A Historical Review

> If you have health, a great craving for adventure, at least a moderate fortune, and can set your heart on a definite object . . . then—travel by all means. [Travelers] explore pasture land in Australia, they hunt for ivory in Africa, they collect specimens of natural history for sale, or they wander as artists.
>
> W. B. Lord and Thomas Baines, 1871[1]

According to Roman mythology, Diana, the goddess of the hunt and the moon, pursued wild game in a variety of celestial and earthly hunting glades. A daughter of Jupiter, and similar to the Greek deity Artemis, she was armed with a bow and arrow and was usually accompanied by a pack of dogs. Once, when the mortal hunter Actaeon spied the goddess as she bathed, Diana angrily turned upon the unfortunate sportsman, transforming him into a stag, whereupon he was savaged by his own hounds.

Non-mythical Dianas have hunted game since time immemorial. Hunting passed from a simple means of survival in prehistoric eras to a leisure activity that separated elite members of society from the masses. It is doubtful women hunters rode in Assyrian chariots of antiquity in pursuit of lions or galloped on horseback over medieval fiefdoms with a hunting falcon perched on a gauntleted fist. However, there were a few who enjoyed the sporting chase. But hunting in bygone eras was almost always confined to the nobility, and women who actually embarked on the trail were undoubtedly rare. It wasn't until the mid–nineteenth century that women, whether well-born or of moderate means, began leaving the safety of hearth and home to travel to distant lands as explorers, adventurers, and big game hunters.

As early as the 1870s, noted African explorer Thomas Baines attempted to describe the motivations that drove individuals to journey to exotic, often hostile regions of a largely unmapped globe. In the heyday of Victorian and Edwardian England, spanning the second half of the nineteenth and the first decades of the twentieth century, most travelers were men seeking to map new territory, extend the boundaries of an empire, or simply search for adventure. The likes of Sir John Franklin, forfeiting his life in pursuit of an Arctic Northwest Passage, and Richard Francis Burton, trekking through unknown Africa in search of the mythical sources of the Nile, provided the impetus for many explorers. As the areas of terra incognitae were explored and mapped, the tentacles of imperialism spread outward from Europe and America, groping toward nearly every corner of the earth.

Travel manuals as prepared by Baines, W. B. Lord, Francis Galton, and Henry Leveson offered insights and suggestions as to what might be encountered on the trail. Based on the experiences of the authors, the manuals were vade mecums for collecting the supplies necessary for a successful expedition or were, at least, encyclopedias concerning the identification and use of native materials to help the struggling traveler or sportsman. Various chapters explored necessary tools, medicines, and firearms. Travelers were instructed how to adopt and adapt to their particular regions of interest. The expedients for building a bridge out of native boats and logs, for instance, were aptly described by Baines in his compendium, as was the construction of igloos in Arctic regions. Galton provided his interpretation of how "to walk a straight line through forests" and even presented a geometric equation on the theory of getting lost.[2]

Women likewise responded to the lure of travel and adventure. While the number of women who traveled and wrote of their observations and experiences was far fewer than that of men, there were still hundreds who broke out of Victorian domesticity and journeyed to the farthest regions of the earth. By the early twentieth century, women responding to the urge to travel were less likely to be considered a novelty. With the growth of the suffrage movement and women's rights carrying to the eve of World War II, even more women took the traveling plunge.

Leaving the safety of home and family for the unknowns of travel has often pegged these women as unconventional. In the nineteenth century, many aristocratic and middle-class women in England, Europe, and the United States were bound by the conventions of matrimony, family duties, and the mediocrity of their private lives. There were, however, a daring few who embarked on travels to escape the monotony of home or simply wanted an adventurous, fulfilling experience. The freedom that travel promised was noted by W. Henry Davenport Adams in his early treatise *Celebrated Women Travellers of the Nineteenth Century* (1883). Burdened by civilization's "restraints, obligations, and responsibilities," Adams wrote, women "should hail even a temporary emancipation through travel."[3] Lilias Campbell Davidson also noted the emancipation of the woman traveler in *Hints to Lady Travellers at Home and Abroad* (1889), that "there is in reality nothing to prevent a woman from seeing every civilized, and even semi-civilized, country in the world without other protection than her own modesty and good sense."[4] Writing more than seventy years later, Dorothy Middleton observed that "travel was an individual gesture of the house-bound, man-dominated Victorian woman. Trained from birth to an almost impossible ideal of womanly submission and self-discipline, of obligation to class and devotion to religion, she had need of an emotional as well as of an intellectual outlet."[5]

The experiences, advice, and insights provided by women travelers in the Victorian Age became a template of sorts for women who trekked abroad in far greater numbers in the twentieth century. In questioning why women, as givers of life, would risk their very lives by venturing abroad, Mary Russell suggested that women needed to enrich their lives, and the "journey must be made which takes them beyond the physical and mental confines set by society . . . that women throughout the centuries have managed to transcend their condition and reach out for the world."[6] It was a transcendent Mary Kingsley who trekked alone through west Africa, for instance, or Fanny Bulloch Workman who scaled the unknown peaks of the Himalayas, then jauntily waved a pro-women's suffrage sign.

Many men, certainly, were less than enthusiastic about seeing women venture from the comforts of hearth and home. The explorer ideal for men was one of fame and fortune, of receiving well-endowed sponsorships, and writing books of their adventures and discoveries. Women, as noted by Dorothy Middleton, were "tolerated rather than encouraged in the field of travel, and then mostly in the subordinate role of wife, guide, or servant."[7] Tolerance was even less on the mind of Sir Clements Markham, then the secretary of the Royal Geographical Society, who remarked that he had "a horror of women of Miss Kingsley's stamp."[8] George Nathaniel Curzon, the Marquess of Curzon, was certain that women's "sex and training render them equally unfit for exploration, and the genus of professional female globe-trotters . . . is one of the horrors of the latter end of the nineteenth century."[9] When it came to recognizing the efforts of women travelers, such prestigious institutions as the Royal Geographical Society and the Royal Scottish Geographical Society generally snubbed them. Curzon, adamantly opposed to the inclusion of women in the RSGC, scathingly remarked: "We contest *in toto* the general capability of women to contribute scientific geographical knowledge."[10] Nor was that discrimination confined to the Old World. With the halls of the Explorers' Club in New York closed to them as late as the 1920s, several American women travelers organized the Society of Women Geographers.

Explorers often turned to big game hunting to quench a scientific thirst through the collection and study of numerous species of wild game from the lands they visited. Collecting game for science meant understanding the nature and habitat of animals, as well as exhibiting personal courage to shoot animals that often turned aggressive if wounded. Taxidermists in London and Europe were kept busy as the flood of animal heads and skins, salted or otherwise preserved, were delivered to their doorsteps from countless international hunting venues. Hunters contributed whole collections of mounted specimens to museums for general audiences to gaze at in wonder.

Scientific curiosity, however, was but one aspect motivating individuals to risk life and limb in the pursuit of big game. Hunting for sport has been a powerful force throughout the development of civilizations. Philosophers have attempted to provide meaning as to why civilized man would seek to kill animals beyond the natural bent of mere survival. Collecting trophies or experiencing exciting moments of the hunt seem to propel *Homo sapiens* back to the roots of humanity. Spanish philosopher José Ortega y Gassett called upon Plato to help define hunting: "Hunting is nothing more than pursuing the game and laying hands on it; as to what is done with that on which one has laid one's hands, once one had laid one's hand on it, this is not pertinent to the hunt."[11] The pursuit Plato notes implies that wild game has a chance to flee or defend itself. Gassett suggests that even though game animals may be faster or stronger than the hunter, the advantage is with the hunter. The actual hunt, then, becomes the effort of foiling the escape or defense of the pursued. Man as hunter calls upon skills, courage, and technology to successfully lay his hand upon the pursued. But Gassett continues that "it is not essential to the hunt that it be successful."[12] He succinctly points out that if the hunter's efforts were "always and inevitably successful it would not be called hunting." The prey occasionally escaping was a necessary element, or as he observes, "the beauty of hunting lies in the fact that it is always problematic."[13] He suggests that man as a predator drops the trappings of civilization to return to his perceptions of an earlier, more natural state: "man, projected by his inevitable progress away from his ancestral proximity to animals, vegetables, and minerals—in sum, to Nature—takes pleasure in the artificial return to it, the only occupation that permits him something like a vacation from his human condition."[14]

It is then, perhaps, that need to return to a "more natural state" that propelled sportsmen to prowl unknown lands with a two-pronged impetus: adventure and sport. While the travel books penned by explorers are legion, there were considerably fewer written concerning big game hunting experiences—perhaps a few thousand, with much fewer than that solely dedicated to hunting.[15] Scott Bennett, in his research on big game hunting in India, discovered that few books written by hunters contained an analysis of why they hunted other than for meat or ivory. What emerges from the sporting works is a body of literature that told an exciting story that partly informed a general readership and also provided details to travelers embarking on military and civil duty in the distant reaches of the empire.[16] A number of books written by participants reflected that blend of duty and leisure activity. Titles such as *Sport and Service in Africa*, by A. H. W. Haywood (1926) and *Leaves from the Diary of a Soldier and Sportsman*, by Montagu Gilbert Gerard (1903) indicate that military service was augmented by the chance to hunt big game.[17] Soldiers on leave were often expected to participate in hunting activities as continued sources of military training. Hugh Gunn, for instance, noted that "the early training and the instincts of the hunter have had much more to do with the expansion of the [British] Empire than is generally recognised."[18] Hunters often equated their experience stalking dangerous game with the same approach as on the battlefield. "Our advance took on much of the routine of trench clearing on the Western Front," wrote Frank Savile of his hunts in British central Africa. "I know I felt positively ethereal."[19]

Non-military sportsmen such as Frederick Courteney Selous, Elim Demidoff, and Charles Sheldon provided the greatest body of big game hunting literature.[20] They, and many others, coupled the essence of the hunt with vivid narratives describing landscapes, native peoples, and fierce battles for survival. Armchair adventurers lapped up the newest printings, reveled in the excitement of the chase in exotic lands, and called for more.

If women as explorers and travelers were relatively few when compared to the number of men who explored and traveled, then women as big game hunters were a rare breed indeed, especially those who wrote of their exploits. Pioneer women, whether on the plains of North America, the frontiers of Asia, or the veldts and forests of Africa, carried arms to defend their families and themselves, and to add to the larder by hunting game. But the need to hunt for survival had changed to hunting for sport by the late nineteenth and early twentieth centuries. Fashionable women in England and Europe participated in shooting game birds such as grouse and pheasant during the great game drives that had become so popular among the elite classes. Dressing in silks for breakfast on the country estates of the privileged, women changed to tweeds to join the menfolk on the afternoon firing line as local villagers and tenant farmers beat the bushes and woods to drive flocks of game birds to the waiting guns. Evening brought frothy baths, expensive gowns, and elaborate dinners as toasts were made and record books noting the number of kills updated.[21]

There was a sophisticated gentility present as some women attempted to emulate men in the grouse butts or pheasant lines . . . and women were expected to copy and strive for the same love and enjoyment of the blood sports as men. Lady Violet Greville noted in her anthology *The Gentlewoman's Book of Sports*:

> A keen love of sport is inherent in the breast of all true Englishmen; and the desire of adventure, the disregard of comfort and danger, that it encourages, have gone far to make them the conquerors of the world . . . The sportsman is not cruel, as has sometimes been wantonly asserted: he loves animals, birds, insects, flowers and all the beauties of nature. In his lonely wanderings face to face with the glorious aspect of sea and sky, of the bleak mountain side and the luxuriant valley, he studies the habits of wild beasts, the ways of feathered fowl, the lore and knowledge of herbs and plants. . . . In like manner, many women have cultivated habits of endurance, of observation, of activity, of courage and self-command, of patience and energy. The record of some of their adventures and pastimes will, I venture to think, be favourably received by the public, and may encourage other women, as feminine but more timid, to imitate their achievements, and to acquire a keen zest for and sympathy with outdoor pursuits.[22]

Greville prefaced a second sporting anthology with additional advice: "When women prove bright and cheerful companions, they add to the man's enjoyment and to the enlarging of their own practical interests."[23] Personal practical interests notwithstanding, if women were to enjoy male activities such as the shooting sports, then they had to conform to male rules.

Men were expected to exude patience and understanding of sportswomen, even if feigned. Missed shots on partridge, grouse, or pheasant could easily be overlooked by male gunners and simply attributed to feminine delicacy and inexperience. Nor would women have to take driven bird shooting too seriously. Baths and clean clothing were never more than a few minutes away. Hunting tweeds and lightweight shotguns could quickly be discarded as the women reentered traditional roles at evening cocktails and dinner.

Hunting big game in Africa, Asia, or the polar regions was far removed, however, from the finery of lavish English and European shooting parties. Few of the popular vade mecums for travelers published in the Victorian era paid any attention to the needs of women abroad. Clothing makers offered few items for women, undoubtedly considering it unladylike for females to hunt big game. When it came to stalking mountain game, Lilias Campbell Davidson suggested that women not accept "the modern feminine costume for mountaineering . . . where the skirt is a mere polite apology—an inch or two below the knee—the result hardly consistent with a high ideal of womanhood."[24] Such an ideal still demanded petticoats and long dresses. Rifle makers, likewise, built firearms suited to male physiques. The sporting challenge for women was to collect trophies or, at very least, to prove that a woman could command an expedition, handle a large-caliber rifle, and bag the requisite animals. The motivations to shoot trophy animals, rarely noted in the books written by women hunters, were undoubtedly the same motivations as for women travelers—to break the social confines of their eras and to enrich themselves with experiences in the big game fields. Laura Franey suggests that "hunting had become firmly established as an arena in which women could prove that they shared with men an instinctual desire for sport and for the kill."[25] Or, as Gassett noted in his *Meditations on Hunting*: "Hunting, like all human occupations, has its different levels, and how little of the real work of hunting is suggested in words like diversion, relaxation, entertainment! A good hunter's way of hunting is a hard job which demands much from man: he must keep himself fit, face extreme fatigues, accept danger."[26] Women's spirit and strength, W. C. Blaikie announced in 1896, "has defied . . . arctic cold and darkness . . . fatigue, hunger and sickness, robbers and extortioners, wild beast, scorpions and mosquitoes, heat and cold, filth and fever, besides the nameless terrors of savage races, on whose whims they could not count, whose greed and ferocity shrank from no crime."[27] As in Blaikie's pronouncement, women proved they were capable of hunting dangerous game in a variety of locations and climatic conditions and facing with the dangers of disease and possible threats from indigenous peoples.

Yet the story of women as big game hunters is virtually unknown. Historical research is practically non-existent. Recent studies of the lives and motivations of women travelers, however, has fared better. Dorothy Middleton provides some depth to the reasons that women traveled but primarily provides biographical accounts of seven women explorers. While Alexandra Allen briefly introduces the world of women travelers, the bulk of her text, like Middleton's, centers on brief biographies of famous women travelers. In her study of Victorian women travel writers in Africa, Catherine Barnes Stevenson not only provides a solid background on women travelers, but also examines travel writing as literature. Both Mary Russell and Dea Birkett make serious attempts at understanding the motivations and experiences of women travelers. Birkett in particular devotes a revealing chapter detailing the difficulties women explorers faced while attempting to gain recognition through the various professional, scientific, and geographical societies proliferating in Victorian England. Analyzing women's travel writing through the lens of feminism, Sara Mills examines the role of women travelers in the broader imperialist culture of the late nineteenth and early twentieth centuries, with the theories of Michel Foucault woven in to provide an evocative literary texture.[28]

Of the few books that mention women as hunters, Jane Robinson's bio-bibliographic guide to women travelers indelicately lumps together a handful of sporting women in a chapter titled "Unfeminine Exploits."[29] In the same vein, Marion Tinling addresses the lives of a number of women travelers in some detail, including several who hunted.[30] Maria Aitken, in her work on the roles played by women travelers, devotes a chapter to "huntresses," though it paints a less-than-flattering picture.[31] Both Bartle Bull and Kenneth Cameron studied the history of big game hunting in Africa, but their mention of women hunters is pedestrian and sparse, Cameron noting that "we know little of the women who led safaris, probably because it has been men who have left most of the records."[32] John M. Mackenzie in his seminal work examining big game hunting, conservation, and British imperialism provides a few paragraphs on women hunters.[33] He also notes that some women turned hunting "into a powerful expression of female emancipation of sorts."[34]

Indeed there is little information regarding women who traveled and hunted. Brief biographical sketches appear in old volumes of *Who's Who*, obituaries, and the occasional reference book on women writers or travelers. Snippets of daily life and experiences can be gleaned from a smattering of letters and documents. The most valuable source of information is the books that women hunters wrote recounting their adventures. Yet these writings, representing "a type of autobiographical narrative," as noted by Catherine Barnes Stevenson, may contain exaggerations or be spiced up to entertain an audience expecting big game hunting thrills.[35] James Casada suggested that African explorers often "dress[ed] up their travelogues with that which was sensational or outré."[36] When comparing the works of men and women hunters, however, the hardships, privations, and dangers they faced are greatly similar.

The content of the books written by women big game hunters generally remained consistent. Occasionally the authors revealed their motivations for traveling and hunting. They chose their rifles, clothing, and supplies, sometimes assembling their own expeditions complete with gun bearers, porters, cooks, and pack animals. Once in the field, women had to contend with cleanliness, usually in a less-than-hospitable climate. Insects and vermin abounded, often carrying fevers or other maladies. The women observed indigenous peoples. The physical hardships of the trail had to be overcome. Encounters with wild animals were challenging and invigorating, yet stressful and often dangerous. What emerged from their writings was a literature revealing women's experiences in an arena combining travel and sport usually reserved for men.

Women were also faced with traveling to the world's shooting grounds either by themselves or accompanied by a spouse or other male friends or family members. Much of the literature of women hunters centers on their location in time and space as wives of soldiers stationed in Africa or Asia at the height of European imperialism. Soldiers or civil servants with a sporting bent might take a wife with them on safari or shikar. Once in the field, women could either remain in camp or join men in the hunt. Usually their role was secondary, with males ensuring that women were not placed in harm's way. Occasionally women embarked on their own hunting expeditions accompanied by only a handful of native guides or porters. In their writings, this latter group of women reveal the richness of personal experience coupled with the resourcefulness and determination as noted by W. C. Blaikie.

In comparing big game books written by women to those penned by men, several generalities become evident. Women tended to be much more descriptive of the actual process of traveling to hunting grounds, including steamship voyages and time spent in foreign cities. Their observations of indigenous peoples, whether viewed through the lens of a perceived superiority or simply through curious eyes, is offered in greater detail, particularly as to how natives interacted within the tribe and how they reacted to white visitors. Women also provided more personal experiences regarding the indelicate nature of going afield, including rudimentary personal hygiene and infestation by vermin. When hunting, women tended to personify the game they stalked with strangely affectionate descriptions, while male hunters were more directly to the point. A common trait of many big game hunting books written by men was a chapter detailing the best rifles and ammunition to use, a subject usually lacking from nearly all women's narratives.[37] The mutual dangers faced by men and women alike were similar, without a doubt. Longtime African hunter and author Denis D. Lyell, noted that he thought the hunter was "in more danger from fevers," and believed "that there is as great a likelihood of meeting one's death from the bite of a poisonous snake as from wild animals."[38] He attributed deaths from animal attacks to four causes: "(1) Recklessness and contempt of danger. (2) Uncertain or long shots. (3) Inferior weapons with insufficient stopping power. (4) Ignorance of the game and its habits."[39] Women's big game encounters reflected Lyell's concerns.

Many of the women who hunted kept diaries or journals or sent letters home, a custom passed without distinction from the Victorian era of the nineteenth century to the eve of World War Two. In revisiting these notebooks or letters months or even years after they were originally penned, women had to reconstruct events in a fluid, literary style that would attract a readership. Their works had to be not only full of adventure but also informative, with a feminine shadowing to attract a female readership in addition to men interested in details of the hunt. Perhaps it is not surprising then that the hunting books written by women were often criticized by reviewers for newspapers and periodicals of their era or soft-pedaled as works delightfully unconventional in their style and approach.

While the bulk of women hunters who wrote of their experiences published books in the mainstream, a few elected to privately print their hunting memoirs, handing them out as gifts or keepsakes to friends and family. Few women provide detail as to why they preferred the small press, but undoubtedly many had reservations as to how the general public would receive their stories. For some, the stigma of a gentlewoman partaking in blood sports was one that they might not have wished to expose publicly.

By 1940, with Europe already embroiled in world war, books about big game hunting seemed to disappear from the literary scene. Traditional maritime travel lanes linking the British Isles, Europe and the United States to the big game grounds of Asia and Africa were no longer safe. Men stationed at colonial outposts were called to duty in various theaters of combat. Women likewise filled important roles in both front line and home front activities. Hunting large game for sport seems to have become a frivolity in the face of the greater death and destruction.[40]

NOTES

1. W. B. Lord and T. Baines, *Shifts and Expedients of Camp Life, Travel & Exploration*, (London: Horace Cox, 1871), p. 7.
2. Francis Galton, *The Art of Travel* (Harrisburg, PA: Stackpole Books, 1971 [1872]), pp. 293–296.

3. W. H. Davenport Adams, *Celebrated Women Travellers of the Nineteenth Century* (London: W. Swan Sonnenschein, 1883), p. 184.

4. Davidson, Lilias Campbell, *Hints to Lady Travellers at Home and Abroad* (London: Iliffe and Son, 1889), p. 1.

5. Dorothy Middleton, *Victorian Lady Travellers* (New York: E. P. Dutton, 1965), p. 4.

6. Mary Russell, *The Blessings of a Good Thick Skirt: Women Travellers and Their World* (London: Collins, 1986), pp. 14–15.

7. Dorothy Middleton, "Women Travellers," *The Discoverers: An Encyclopedia of Explorers and Exploration*, ed. Helen Delpar (New York: McGraw-Hill, 1980), p. 457.

8. Quoted in Middleton, "Women Travellers," p. 460.

9. "Women Travellers" p. 460.

10. Quoted in Alexandra Allen, *Travelling Ladies* (London: Jupiter, 1980), pp. 11–12.

11. José Ortega y Gassett, *Meditations on Hunting* (New York: Charles Scribner's Sons, 1972), p. 56.

12. Gassett, *Meditations on Hunting*, p. 57

13. Gassett, *Meditations on Hunting*, p. 58.

14. Gassett, *Meditations on Hunting*, p. 129.

15. Kenneth P. Czech, *An Annotated Bibliography of African Big Game Hunting Books, 1785–1950* (St. Cloud, MN: Land's Edge Press, 1999). More than 600 titles with African big game hunting content were compiled. To date, there are no other bibliographies solely addressing big game hunting in other continents.

16. Scott Bennett, "Shikar and the Raj," *South Asia* (1984), p. 72.

17. A. H. W. Haywood, *Sport and Service in Africa* (London: Seeley, Service, 1926); Montagu Gilbert Gerard, *Leaves from the Diaries of a Soldier and Sportsman* (New York: E. P. Dutton, 1903).

18. Hugh Gunn, "The Sportsman as an Empire Builder," *Empire Big Game* (London: Simpkin, Marshall, Hamilton, Kent, & Co., 1925), p. 1.

19. Frank Savile, *The High Grass Trail* (London: H.F. & G. Witherby, 1924), p. 111.

20. Frederick Selous (1851–1917) a British subject, was an authority on hunting in Africa; Elim Demidoff (1868–?) a Russian aristocrat, hunted on the frontiers of the Russian empire; Charles Sheldon (1867–1928) was an American who specialized in hunting in the Alaskan wilderness. Each wrote several popular books of travel and sport.

21. See Jonathan Garnier Ruffer, *The Big Shots: Edwardian Shooting Parties* (London: Debrett-Viking Press, 1977) for descriptions of the lavish hunts in the British Isles. See also Lord Ralph Percy, *Debrett's Book of Game Cards* (London: Debrett's Peerage, 1986) for details regarding the elaborate game cards kept by sportsmen during estate shoots.

22. Lady Greville (ed.), *The Gentlewoman's Book of Sports* (London: Henry and Co., no date), pp. 5–6.

23. Lady Greville (ed.), *Ladies in the Field: Sketches of Sport* (London: W. Thacker, 1900), p. iv.

24. Davidson, Hints to *Lady Travellers*, p. 154.

25. Laura Franey, "Violent Equality: A Reappraisal of Travel and Fin-de-Siecle Feminism," paper presented at the Snapshots Abroad Conference, University of Minnesota (November 14–16, 1997).

26. Gassett, *Meditations on Hunting*, p. 31

27. W. C. Blaikie, "Lady Travellers," *Blackwood's Magazine* (1896), p. 49.

28. Middleton, *Victorian Lady Travellers*; Alexandra Allen, *Travelling Ladies* (London: Jupiter, 1980); Catherine Barnes Stevenson, *Victorian Women Travel Writers in Africa* (Boston: Twayne, 1982); Mary Russell, *The Blessings of a Good Thick Skirt* (London: Collins, 1986); Dea Birkett, *Spinsters Abroad* (New York: Basil Blackwell, 1989); Sara Mills, *Discourses of Difference* (London: Routledge, 1991).

29. Jane Robinson, *Wayward Women* (Oxford: Oxford University Press, 1990), pp. 62–63. Interestingly, Robinson also includes women mountaineers and bicyclists in her chapter "Unfeminine Exploits."

30. Marion Tinling, *Women into the Unknown: A Sourcebook on Women Explorers and Travelers* (Westport, CT: Greenwood, 1989).

31. Maria Aitken, *A Girdle Around the Earth* (London: Constable, 1987), p. 85. Aitken admits in her "Foreword" that the only woman in her book she strongly disliked was Agnes Herbert (see chapter 5).

32. Kenneth Cameron, *Into Africa: The Story of the East African Safari*, (London: Constable, 1990), p. 75; Bartle Bull, *Safari: A Chronicle of Adventure* (New York: Viking, 1988).

33. John M. Mackenzie, *The Empire of Nature* (Manchester: Manchester University Press, 1988).

34. John M. Mackenzie, "The Imperial Pioneer and Hunter and the British Masculine Stereotype in Late Victorian and Edwardian Times," *Manliness and Morality: Middle-class Masculinity in Britain and America, 1800–1940* (New York: St. Martins Press, 1987), p. 179.

35. Stevenson, *Victorian Women Travel Writers*, p. 3.

36. James Casada, "Literature and Exploration," *The Discoverers: An Encyclopedia of Explorers and Exploration*, ed. Helen Delpar (New York: McGraw-Hill, 1980), p. 16.

37. Czech, *An Annotated Bibliography of African Big Game Hunting Books.* In studying more than six hundred books containing African big game hunting, I compared the general writing style of male writers to that of female writers.

38. Denis D. Lyell, *Wild Life in Central Africa* (London: The Field & Queen, 1913), p. 211.

39. Lyell, p. 80.

40. Czech, *An Annotated Bibliography of African Big Game Hunting*. Of the more than 600 books compiled, fewer than a dozen were published from 1939 to 1950, and all of them except two privately printed works contained big game hunting prior to World War II.

TWO

Victorian Dianas

"Women who prefer exercise and liberty, who revel in the cool sea breeze, and love to feel the fresh mountain air fanning their cheeks, who are afraid neither of a little fatigue nor of a little exertion, are the better, the truer, and the healthier, and can yet remain essentially feminine in their thoughts and manners."[1]

Lady Greville

Lady Violet Greville's paean to the exuberance of women involved in outdoor activities mentioned nothing of the inherent dangers of the sport of big game hunting. A decidedly male activity, stalking dangerous game was not for the faint of heart. The trip alone to the hunting grounds was a strenuous experience, not to mention facing the charge of a wounded beast. A woman, after all, couldn't be expected to emulate the exploits of Victorian sportsman William Cornwallis Harris or the powerful Scotsman Gordon Rouleyn Cumming, both of whom spent months at a time in Africa's bush country and killed hundreds of heads of game with muzzle-loading rifles. What woman could handle the likes of Samuel White Baker's massive four-bore rifle that spun even that intrepid explorer about when he fired it? There were also the matters of disease, unhygienic conditions, lack of privacy, and the vagaries of climate and topography to consider. Few husbands or fathers would consider subjecting their spouse or daughter to the dangers of primitive lands. Small wonder then that only a handful of nineteenth-century women ventured on the hunting trails.

Some Victorian women, though, did seek adventure in the haunts of big game but rarely wrote of their exploits. Fanny Eden, for instance, spent eighteen months in northern India in the mid-1830s and took part in a tiger hunt from elephant back. The journals of her adventures and observations, however, were not published until 1988, and she tended to be more observer than participant. Fanny Parkes, another Indian traveler from the 1840s, mentions only a few sporting incidents in her book. Florence Baker spent several years in central Africa with her husband, noted big game hunter and explorer Sir Samuel White Baker. Her diaries, recounting the years 1870–1873, were first published in 1972 but reveal no hunting exploits. Katherine Petherick, a contemporary of Florence Baker's, co-authored a book with husband John Petherick of their African adventure, but with no hunting on her part. Considering the primitive and dangerous state of Africa at the time, and that both Sam Baker and John Petherick were skilled sportsmen, it is reasonable to assume that Florence and Katherine hunted as well but elected to keep those experiences to themselves. In the cases of these four women, sport was not at the root of their travels. It may well be that these Victorians simply didn't want the notoriety of enjoying a blood sport, or that their in-print exposure to the dangers of the hunt might have reflected badly on their husbands or other male relatives, who could be considered lax in their protection of women.[2]

As more women began traveling abroad, whether accompanied by relatives and friends or going alone, a few decided to tote rifles and shotguns and enjoy sport on their journey. In choosing rifles for big game hunting, women were faced with a variety of shooting and gun-fitting problems. Stalking dangerous animals such as rhinoceroses, elephants, and buffalo required rifles of large caliber capable of delivering heavy bullets designed to "shock" or stop a charging beast in its tracks. Books for travelers, such as *Shifts and Expedients of Camp Life* (1871) argued for large-bore rifles and provided detailed analysis of firing proper loads.[3] Francis Galton, an experienced African explorer and hunter, advocated in *The Art of Travel* (1872) that small-bore guns were insufficient for most game: "For the larger kinds of game, such as elephants and buffaloes, experienced sportsmen mostly prefer guns of immense bore, carrying round bullets that weighed a quarter of a pound. The recoil is tremendous, and would injure the shoulder if the sportsman did not use a pad against which he rests the gun. The guns must be strong, because very large charges of powder are invariably used where great power of penetration is required."[4]

Cartridges for massive four-, eight-, and ten-bore rifles were packed with heavy charges of black powder. A four-bore rifle, for instance, firing a conical bullet weighing 1,882 grams and needing twelve drams of powder, generated more than 6,000 foot-pounds of striking energy at a range of fifty yards—the power of penetration Galton noted.[5] Recoil from such behemoths could punish even the most ardent and experienced of men, let alone women. Smaller .40- and .45-caliber rifles of the Victorian era, calibers often favored by women, offered reduced recoil but at the expense of "shocking" power. By the twentieth century, however, faster-burning and more efficient gunpowders allowed lighter-caliber rifles to deliver their bullets with both speed and power.

Finding a rifle to fit the anatomy of a woman also presented various problems. Most rifles built for big game hunting in Africa and Asia were constructed for men. During the building process, gunmakers measured the length of the shooter's arm, shoulder span, and neck to ensure that the finished product fit the individual as a suit of clothes might. As the rifle was crafted, the shooter's dimensions were incorporated into the fashioning of the stock. Under most circumstances, the measurements of the stock built for a man simply did not fit many women comfortably. Prior to embarking on an expedition, women had to make sure their guns fit properly by either having them built to their own specifications (a time-consuming and expensive process) or having existing rifles modified.

CORNELIA MARY SPEEDY

Cornelia Mary Speedy carried a Swiss-made Fetterlich rifle fitted with a hair trigger on her expedition with her husband to the Sudan. Married to British army captain Charles Speedy, she accompanied him to his assignment in the Malay Peninsula in the early 1870s. In 1878 the couple departed Penang for a shooting expedition to Africa. Charlie Speedy had hoped to hunt in Abyssinia (modern Ethiopia), where he had served earlier in his career, but current political turmoil forced him to opt for the eastern Sudan. During their journey, Cornelia Speedy penned a number of letters to her mother in England. Among the more than three tons of luggage accompanying the expedition were boxes of tools, arsenical supplies for preserving trophies, and three tents, one of which she had cut out of cloth and stitched on her own sewing machine. Her tents featured bedrooms and separate compartments for the baths.

Choosing clothing for the journey was especially difficult for Speedy, as few women had traveled in and written about the region. In the end she chose a large pith hat with "a very broad brim, and a thick gauze veil doubled over it and tied carefully down" to keep sand from blowing in her face.[6] Tucked around her neck was a large silk handkerchief. While she chose long Victorian dresses for everyday travel, she also included a white frilled dressing gown, which she luxuriated in during the late-afternoon and evening hours of camp. For footwear, she chose Balmorals, high-laced boots rising above the ankle.

The Sudan of the era was an inhospitable place for a Victorian woman. Clouds of biting gnats forced Mrs. Speedy to defend herself with spirits of camphor, eau de cologne, and even spirits of peppermint. She likened the harsh, baking east winds beating against the exposed skin of her face to the blast from a great furnace. "My face is dreadfully burnt and my lips are fearfully sore," she wrote in a letter, "and though I scarcely like to confess it, I have not been able to touch my face with water for the last two days, for it is almost raw, the skin having nearly all peeled off."[7] Using a silk handkerchief to dab away the dust from her tortured face, she rubbed in pure neat's-foot oil, which her husband used to lubricate his hunting rifles. No wonder, then, that the rare pleasures of the bath via an inflatable tub meant so much to her: "You would have to come into the Sudan, or some other uncivilized land, and go through the same sort of travelling that we have been doing of late, before you could realise the heavenly enjoyment of a bath, fresh clothes, and a clean white morning wrapper."[8]

With a parasol over her shoulder, Cornelia Speedy learned to ride a camel and scout herds of antelope. It was her encounter with curious native Sudanese, however, that left an indelible impression on her. Upon reaching a village, her high-laced shooting boots became the subject of much conversation and touching by local tribesmen. Her ability to act as an impromptu seamstress to repair her torn garments also awed the Sudanese. When she wrote in her journals or letters, a number of tribal elders not only observed her doing so but also questioned her husband. "They [the village men] had not previously believed that a woman could achieve that art, and probably entertained doubts as to the amount of mischief she might not be able to perpetrate if she could wield such a power," she wrote. "They asked Charlie with unmistakable anxiety if all women in his country could write; and when he replied that there were very few indeed who could not, they shook their heads, and felt . . . that it was a land they were safer away from!"[9] Later, near the Setit River, a group of native women suddenly confronted Mrs. Speedy, plucking at her silk handkerchief, trying to turn up the sleeves of her tunic, and grabbing at her buttons. After her initial panic, she discovered the Sudanese women were only trying to determine if she actually had white skin *under* her clothing.

As the Speedys neared the end of their expedition, a savage thunderstorm threatened their caravan. As night fell, thick clouds began building. Racing to pitch their tents and secure their supplies and trophies, the Speedys and their porters were suddenly doused by torrential rains. Within minutes, a flash flood swept their campsite. Boxes, bags, and bales were carried away by the torrent. Fighting the rising water, Cornelia and Charlie managed to free their animals from where they had been tethered. "I shall never forget that walk . . . not above a hundred yards, for I thought I should never get there," she penned in a letter to her mother. "The surface of the ground, which had been baked to a dry brittle crust, scarcely thicker than an oatmeal biscuit, was now one mass of slime; it was two steps forward and one back the whole way."[10] Fortunately, the Speedys and their porters survived with only the loss of a few supplies and animals.

Upon their return to England, Cornelia Speedy collected the letters she had sent home and edited them into her two-volume *My Wanderings in the Soudan* (1884). The book, complete with the couple's travels, adventures, and descriptions of Charlie's hunts after big game, only briefly mentioned her own hunting experiences. It was typical that the woman downplays her role when compared to her spouse.

While Speedy wrote of her adventures in Africa, it was India where Victorian women in the heyday of the British Raj enjoyed sport the most. English sahibs had hunted tiger and other game for decades. It was only natural that memsahibs with an adventurous bent follow suit. Hunting parties ranged from simple affairs of individual stalking of animals, of waiting on raised shooting platforms called *machans* for passing game, to elaborate game drives with local villagers literally beating the bushes to frighten game animals toward shooters perched in howdahs on elephant back. As was the case with many Victorian-era women hunters, the women accompanied their husbands for the purpose of a vacation or because the spouse was stationed as a military officer or civil servant in that portion of the empire.

MRS. RICHARD H. TYACKE

Among the women who hunted in India was Mrs. Richard Humphrey Tyacke. A veteran of hunts in Albania and Kashmir, Tyacke and her husband, a renowned sportsman and colonel in the British army, traveled into the foothills of the northwestern Himalayas in pursuit of bears, ibex, and other game. Little is known of her early life, though one author has suggested that the Tyackes were not legally married.[11]

At barely five feet tall, Mrs. Tyacke had to adapt her conventional English outdoors clothing as well as her native Indian garments to both fit her frame and meet the challenges of mountain weather:

> I wore a very short plain skirt of the strong *karkee* drill, such as soldiers wear in India, and a Norfolk jacket of the same material. The skirt was not too narrow, or it would have interfered with the jumping and climbing over rocks that is so often necessary. On the legs I wore stockings with feet cut off, on the feet short worsted socks with *puttoo* (homespun) over-socks, and grass shoes. Bound round the legs I wore the grey *putties* of India, which are strips of *puttoo* four and a half inches long, by four and a half inches wide. The advantage of wearing *karkee* is, that the color is so admirably suited for sport, and that it never tears. Although it sounds cold, and undoubtedly *is* cold, that difficulty can be overcome by wearing plenty of underclothing. A further advantage is that *karkee* can be easily washed, which was a consideration, as I had often to wash part of my own clothing.[12]

In addition, she included a grey *puttoo* jacket, a small cap, and warm gloves when hunting above the snow line. A gray felt Terai hat was her choice for head covering under a tropical sun. Shoes of woven grass bound across the foot and between the toes were often worn when stalking among the rocks. When in camp, Mrs. Tyacke enjoyed wearing a cardigan jacket, short *puttoo* skirts and leather sandals and warned that chill nights required a warm sleeping jacket and pajamas.

Tyacke and her husband spent several shooting seasons in the Kashmiri highlands. Winter snows gave way to sleet, drenching downpours, and the occasional dust storm. Legions of blue bottle flies and ticks abounded. When cholera struck the surrounding region, the shooting party opted to move to Lahoul, where they expected the greater altitude and extreme cold to protect them. She provided ample details of their excursions in Lahoul, with observations of native life and of Buddhist lamas. In one village, she was presented with the cub of a snow leopard. Feeding the cub proved a challenge as she resorted to milk in a sponge, from a bit of rubber tubing, and from a glove with a tiny hole cut in the thumb. When none of those alternatives worked, she tried to have the leopard nurse at a goat. When that failed, she finally experienced success with a spoon. Ultimately, Mrs. Tyacke admitted that the cub had no place in their camp and had it sent to an Englishman's home in the Kullu Valley.

While travel provided many interesting vignettes, the Tyackes much preferred sporting adventures. Armed with a doubled-barreled .400 Express rifle by Holland of London, and a .410 shotgun by Cheltenham for bird shooting, Mrs. Tyacke chose to be in the woods in company with her husband or hunting alone. The first season of shooting in the Kullu district netted the couple hundreds of pheasant and partridges, as well as more than a dozen bears; a bag, Mrs. Tyacke noted, that "might have been considerably increased, had we cared to go in for the slaughter."[13] She often hired entire villages to beat the surrounding jungle and hills to drive big game to waiting hunters. While the practice was relatively widespread, in some cases too many beaters spoiled the hunt. On one occasion, she recalled how several promising bear-hunting adventures were ruined by the presence of large numbers of villagers who ranged through the forest beating their drums or discharging their own primitive firearms. A furious Tyacke revealed it was nearly impossible to keep the beaters in a line if a bear had been spotted: "They move about the jungle in gangs, each trying to get the other to go in front, and utterly regardless of direction, while they decline to face the thickest and most likely cover."[14] She was prompt to reward villagers, however, if they spotted game that resulted in a kill.

If Cornelia Speedy was somewhat reticent in describing her personal hunts in the Sudan, Mrs. Tyacke seemed to revel in the adventure. While hunting bears above the snow line of India's Kullu Valley, she wounded a bruin, then watched it race downhill toward a snow-covered river as she fumbled to reload her rifle. As the bear sped across the stream, it disappeared through a hole in the snow and ice. With her shikari in tow, Tyacke stalked along the river banks, hoping to find another hole that would reveal the animal. After they had passed several openings, the bear suddenly kicked up through the ice and clambered toward them. She coolly dispatched it with a single shot.[15]

After spending nearly two years in Kullu and Lahoul in northern India, the Tyackes returned to England with Mrs. Tyacke sporting a specially made *kirkitzee*, a head ornament from Lahoul worn only by married women. Both took up the pen. The colonel's book, a guide to hunting in northern India, was published in 1893 in Calcutta.[16] Mrs. Tyacke preferred capturing her personal adventures in detail in *How I Shot My Bears*, printed later that year in London.

KATE MARTELLI

Kate Martelli, a contemporary of Tyacke's, also traveled to India in the early 1890s. Accompanied by her husband, she was invited to shoot in a variety of locales in northern and central India. As with Tyacke, little is known of her beyond her skill as a tiger hunter. Upon her first invitation to hunt on a maharaja's private grounds, she worried about what clothing she should wear. Deciding upon cotton, she provided her tailor with a length of material to transform into a proper shooting dress. By morning her attire was finished: a loose-fitting dress dyed green with a green cotton cover camouflaging her Terai sun helmet.

Upon arriving at the shooting grounds, Martelli proudly displayed her rifle: "My weapon was a .450 double express rifle, by Alex Henry."[17] Her Henry would serve admirably as she hunted tigers not only from a howdah-mounted elephant but also from a stone tower, a rocky ledge, and an open field crisscrossed by ravines. From the ledge turned shooting platform, she and her husband were charged by a tiger. For a moment, she froze, admiring the speeding animal, before she and her husband fired simultaneously. When the tiger continued its attack, she emptied her remaining barrel. With scant seconds to reload, she fired yet a third round as the big cat scrabbled at the base of the ledge and was momentarily lost from sight. "We did not dare, of course, to come down from our rock, as we had no idea where he was, or to what extent he was crippled," she admitted. When the local maharaja finally approached on elephant back, the tiger was found severely wounded among a jumble of rocks at the foot of the ledge and soon dispatched.[18] Kate Martelli's record of bagging five tigers was captured in "Tigers I Have Shot," a chapter she contributed to Lady Violet Greville's anthology, *Ladies in the Field: Sketches of Sport* (1900).

NORA BEATRICE GARDNER

Nora Beatrice Gardner, the eldest daughter of Lord Blyth of Blythwood, was another visitor to India, the jewel in the British imperialist crown. Married to Alan Gardner, a member of Parliament, she traveled with her husband on a variety of sporting trips to Canada, Australia, and the interiors of Somalia and Abyssinia. A mother of two, though one child died at a young age, Gardner enjoyed an unlikely combination of recreations including gardening, embroidery, cooking, sketching, and big game hunting.

In October 1892, the Gardners arrived in India after a leisurely cruise. Nora Gardner noted her experiences and sketched her observations in a journal she maintained in minute detail. Traveling by horseback and coach by day, she and her husband visited a number of Indian towns and palaces of local maharajas. At night they often took lodging in native huts. On one rainy evening, in the hill country of Nurpoor in northern India, their sojourn was interrupted by a swarm of large hornets. "Looking above, the walls and roof were festooned with hundreds of venomous-looking insects," she noted in her journal later that night. Gardner was stung, and despite "a brisk slaughter, all hands busily engaged with shoes and slippers," the hornets carried the engagement, driving the hut's human inhabitants into the rain.[19]

The primary purpose of the trip to India, however, was to enjoy sport, including that most famous of Indian field sports—pig sticking. Pig sticking, in which mounted men and women armed with lances chased wild boars, required iron nerves, equestrian skills, and a strong arm. During one pig sticking engagement in the Rajpoot district, Nora Gardner elected to be an observer rather than participant. As a powerful boar dashed past the line of horsemen, Gardner suddenly found herself the pig's target. Unarmed, she gave spurs to her steed as the boar plunged toward her. Fortunately, her husband managed to bridge the distance between boar and wife, spearing the animal from behind.

Nonplussed by the incident, Mrs. Gardner was ready to take up the rifle in pursuit of game. To ensure that the memsahib could handle a rifle properly before venturing to his private hunting grounds, the Maharaja of Chamba arranged a shooting exhibition. A caged leopard was released a few hundred yards away from the shooting party. Nervously, in front of many spectators, she drew her rifle to her shoulder, aimed, and fired. Although the leopard bounded away, the male members of her party, including her husband, politely declared that she had registered a hit. When other shooters finally dropped the leopard, a quick examination proved that her .450 bullet had indeed struck the feline. "I had the satisfaction of knowing that I really had not missed," crowed an elated Mrs. Gardner.[20] Though she had helped dispatch the leopard, her subsequent outing was less than successful. While stalking urials, a species of wild sheep, she missed with her first shot and was unable to fire a second. Mahomet, her new *shikari*, or hunting guide, "could not conceal his disgust and disappointment."[21]

After spending the winter in northern India, the Gardners returned to London, where some of their trophies would soon decorate their home. Nora Gardner penned *Rifle and Spear with the Rajpoots* (1895), apologizing to her readers that her book was "simply a plain and unvarnished account of our rough but very pleasant experience of Indian Camp Life."[22] In traditional Victorian fashion, she downplayed her own sporting activities, though including a number of her husband's adventures taken verbatim from his diary. Apparently Mrs. Gardner gave up big game shooting and became involved in liberal political activities. She was vice president of the Women's Liberal Federation for England and chaired a number of charitable organizations. Nora Gardner died in 1944.

ISABEL SAVORY

Travel writer Isabel Savory wrote three popular titles but only one concerning her big game hunting activities. Born in Weybridge, Surrey, in 1869, she enjoyed numerous outdoor activities including golf and fox-hunting. Unlike Cornelia Speedy, Mrs. Tyacke, and other Victorian women big game hunters who rarely expressed why they traveled and hunted, Savory attempted to identify her new passion of trekking abroad. "*I have felt* stands for more than *I can imagine what others have felt,*" she noted. "Experience means a variety of things: it includes the development of the perceptive powers, dependence upon self, and a wider knowledge of self . . . it causes, in short, a great mental expansion."[23] The hunting fields of India were but one place where she could expand her experiences.

Accompanied by several English male and female friends, Savory embarked on a tour of the subcontinent. Her efforts took her among the snow-covered peaks of Kashmir, where she slept with all her clothes and boots on not only to fight the cold but also to be ready should heavy snowfalls snap the bamboo poles of her tent. Later, when her hunting party descended into jungle lowlands to hunt tigers, the temperature soared to 115 degrees. "I used to soak a handkerchief in water and put it in the crown of my *topi*, resoaking it at every pool of water we ever came across, even though it was very far from cold," she wrote.[24]

Savory refused to give up the long skirts of her era in lieu of shorter garments or knickerbockers, which were slowly coming into fashion. Used to arranging her skirts to ride sidesaddle, she was uncomfortable when forced to ride astride the horse on a man's saddle. While riding along narrow Himalayan passes, she constantly had to loosen her skirt from the pommel. On one occasion, she had just freed the material when her mount's hind legs suddenly kicked out loose rocks. With her horse screaming in terror as its legs buckled on the sheer-edged path, Savory managed to slip from the saddle just as her steed plunged to its death. "But for the facts that I had just happened to pull out my skirt, and, being on a man's saddle, slipped off at once, the rocky gorge would have held us side by side," she shakily observed.[25]

Once free of the lofty recesses of the hill country, Savory preferred clothing made of *puttoo*, *a la* Mrs. Tyacke, though she eschewed Tyacke's grass shoes for boots fitted with India-rubber soles, noting that the grass thongs between the toes were an aggravation. While she occasionally sported a tweed hat for tiger stalking, her preferred headgear was a broad-brimmed solá topi, more resembling a large beehive than a sun helmet. Sewn into her jacket were pads to protect her shoulder from her rifle's recoil. In addition, she wore "dogskin gloves, minus half the fingers" to better grasp the hot barrels of her rifle.[26]

Savory followed an itinerary that included visiting many famous locations and historical sites in India. Though she was an accomplished observer of architecture and customs, she abhorred constant sight-seeing, preferring action and adventure superimposed over breathtaking scenery. If it meant discomfort to take advantage of adventurous opportunities, Savory meant to plunge in. She didn't feel she was unique in her desire: "every year, women who come out, and who travel over the globe, with the object of seeing other sides of that interesting individual, man, other corners of the world, other occupations, and other sports," were increasing in numbers.[27]

With British imperial power at its zenith, women travelers often espoused the cause of European imperialism with its self-justifications of superiority and morality. While in Peshawar, Savory noted that the streets of the bazaars were crowded with a variety of ethnic groups, many men armed with curved daggers at their belts. "One realizes at once what it is to be the only Englishwoman among thousands of natives," she observed. "Every eye is on you . . . the secret of British power in the East is that they have no fear."[28] British fearlessness notwithstanding, Savory was only too glad to return to the safety of the English cantonment in the city.

Action and adventure, however, were foremost in the minds of the little knot of English travelers accompanying Savory. In a not-uncommon literary ploy, she referred to her partners only by an initial. Thus, among her friends was another young woman known simply as M. Of similar adventurous bent as Savory, M. indulged in pig sticking on the estate of the Maharaja of Bahadur, an episode that nearly cost her her life when an enraged boar slashed her jacket with its tusks after she was unhorsed. Clambering among Kashmiri hills and ravines, she bagged several bears, including one that attacked her, and made a difficult shot on an escaping tahr, a species of Himalayan wild goat.

Not to be outdone by M., Savory also stalked tahrs. Several trophy tahrs had bounded up the mountainside as her party approached, so there was little they could do except follow them across the treacherous landscape. After climbing over jutting rock piles and narrow ledges, Savory found herself on the mountain's north face, where a sheet of soft snow stretched before her. Pursuing the goat, she and her shikaris plunged into the snow, often sinking past their knees. With fingers and toes numbed, she tried to move as quietly as possible lest the wily goat dash away. She spied the animal at various distances, then finally located the tahr feeding on a patch of grass on the opposite side of a ravine. Before she could fire, the goat ambled beyond another ridge. As she edged toward it, it suddenly broke cover and sped across her path. Before she could bring her rifle up, one of her companions bagged it with a well-placed shot. Trophy-less, a disconsolate Savory returned to camp.

If she failed to bag bears or tahrs, Savory proved herself an able tiger hunter. Perched in a machan in the scrub forests of the Deccan, she waited in temperatures in excess of 100 degrees for beaters to drive the tigers toward her and her companions. Stifling heat and windless nights did not deter her from continuing her post. When tigers finally crashed through the brush toward her, she managed to dispatch three. "Do not set out on a tiger shoot without being prepared for a great deal of discomfort . . . which amount sometimes almost to purgatory," she warned. "Unless a woman is physically strong, it would be foolhardiness to spend eight weeks under such conditions. But, after all, it is worth it, and a high price has to be paid because it is worth it."[29]

Isabel Savory returned to London where she wrote a description of her travels and adventures in *A Sportswoman in India* (1900). The work combined historical perspectives, sight-seeing, and, above all, sporting exploits. She had also gained a healthy appreciation of the importance of travel in regard to understanding and accepting the cultures of other lands:

> Travel teaches us to see over our boundary fences, to think less intolerantly, less contemptuously of each other. It teaches us to overlook the limitations of religions and morality, and to recognise that they are relative terms, fluctuating quantities, husks round the kernel of truth. Travel dismisses the notion that we are each of us the biggest dog in the kennel.[30]

By 1901, Savory was once more on the trail, this time traveling on horseback with her friend Rose Chamberlain through the Atlas Mountains into Morocco. Apparently, she had abandoned her big game hunting interest and preferred the role of observer and tourist. Her trip to North Africa was described in her second book, *In the Tail of the Peacock* (1903). Savory's third record of travel wouldn't appear in print until 1919. *The Romantic Rousillon* was a rather passive account of a jaunt into the French Pyrenees.

Far more Victorian women accompanied their husbands on shooting trips and remained virtually anonymous. Sophie Demidoff traveled with her husband, Russian aristocrat Prince Elim Demidoff, on hunting expeditions to the Altai Mountains of Mongolia and the Kamchatka Peninsula of Russia's east coast. Elim Demidoff never mentioned his wife by name throughout his description of the Mongolian expedition, even though she borrowed his hunting companion's rifle and fired at several wild sheep. He did, however, gallantly dedicate his book *A Shooting Trip to Kamchatka* (1904) to her and named a remote Kamchatkan lake after her. Likewise, the wife of famous English sportsman St. George Littledale traveled with him on numerous hunts in Kashmir, the Caucasus, Mongolia, and the Pamirs but received scant attention. Henry Zouch Darrah's spouse journeyed with him on his shooting expeditions to Kashmir, Baltistan, and Tibet but is referred to only as his "wife" and seemed not to be included in any sport. Unless a woman was willing to write of her experiences herself, apparently, she would receive short shrift in works written by others.[31]

NOTES

1. Lady Greville ed., *Ladies in the Field: Sketches of Sport* (London: W. Thacker, 1900), pp. iii–iv.

2. Fanny Eden, *Tigers, Durbars and Kings: Fanny Eden's Indian Journals 1837–1838* (London: John Murray, 1988); Fanny Parkes, *Wanderings of a Pilgrim* (London: Pelham Richardson, 1850); Anne Baker ed., *Morning Star: Florence Baker's Diary of the Expedition to Put Down the Slave Trade on the Nile, 1870–73* (London: William Kimber, 1972); Mr. and Mrs. Petherick, *Travels in Central Africa* (London: Tinsley Brothers, 1869).

3. W. B. Lord and T. Baines, *Shifts and Expedients of Camp Life, Travel & Exploration* (London: Horace Cox, 1871), pp. 9–17.

4. Francis Galton, *The Art of Travel* (Harrisburg, PA: Stackpole Books, 1971 [1872]), p. 238.

5. George A. Hoyem, *The History and Development of Small Arms Ammunition*, Vol. 3: British Sporting Rifle (Tacoma, WA: Armory Publications, 1985), p. 7.

6. Mrs. Charles Speedy, *My Wanderings in the Soudan*, vol. 1 (London: Richard Bentley, 1884), p. 63.

7. Mrs. Speedy, *My Wanderings in the Soudan*, v. 1, p. 63.

8. Mrs. Speedy, *My Wanderings in the Soudan*, v. 1, p. 141.

9. Mrs. Speedy, *My Wanderings in the Soudan*, v. 1, p. 98.

10. Mrs. Speedy, *My Wanderings in the Soudan*, v. 2, p. 205.

11. Jane Robinson, *Wayward Women* (Oxford: Oxford University Press, 1990), p. 77.

12. Mrs. R. H. Tyacke, *How I Shot My Bears* (London: Sampson Low, Marston & Company, 1893), pp. 43–45.

13. Mrs. Tyacke, *How I Shot My Bears*, p. 16.

14. Mrs. Tyacke, *How I Shot My Bears*, p. 32.

15. Mrs. Tyacke, *How I Shot My Bears*, p. 62.

16. R. H. Tyacke, *The Sportsman's Manual* (Calcutta: Thacker & Spink, 1893). It was reprinted in 1927.

17. Kate Martelli, "Tigers I Have Shot," *Ladies in the Field: Sketches of Sport* (London: W. Thacker, 1900), p. 147.

18. Kate Martelli, pp. 151–152.

19. Mrs. Alan Gardner, *Rifle and Spear with the Rajpoots* (London: Chatto & Windus, 1895), p. 177.

20. Mrs. Gardner, *Rifle and Spear with the Rajpoots*, p. 128.

21. Mrs. Gardner, *Rifle and Spear with the Rajpoots*, p. 184.

22. Mrs. Gardner, *Rifle and Spear with the Rajpoots*, p. ix.

23. Isabel Savory, *A Sportswoman in India* (London: Hutchinson, 1900), p. 404.

24. Isabel Savory, *A Sportswoman in India*, p. 277.

25. Isabel Savory, *A Sportswoman in India*, p. 142.

26. Isabel Savory, *A Sportswoman in India*, p. 256.

27. Isabel Savory, *A Sportswoman in India.*

28. Isabel Savory, *A Sportswoman in India*, p. 56.

29. Isabel Savory, *A Sportswoman in India*, pp. 282–283.

30. Isabel Savory, *A Sportswoman in India*, p. 404.

31. E. Demidoff, *After Wild Sheep in the Altai and Mongolia* (London: Rowland Ward, 1900); Demidoff, *A Shooting Trip to Kamchatka* (London: Rowland Ward, 1904); for various contributions by St. George Littledale, see *The Badminton Library: Big Game Shooting*, Vol. 2 (London: Longmans, Green, 1894); Henry Zouch Darrah, *Sport in the Highlands of Kashmir* (London: Rowland Ward, 1896).

THREE

Florence Dixie: Victorian in the Southern Hemisphere

"I realized that my sex was the barrier that hid from my yearning gaze the bright fields of activity, usefulness and reform."[1]

Lady Florence Dixie, 1891

As Victorian women proved, there were few places they could not venture. Mary Kingsley, garbed in full skirts, trod boldly through west Africa. Kate Marsden traveled by horseback, by sleigh, and on foot to visit leper colonies in Siberia. Fanny Bullock Workman gained considerable prestige from her climbs in the Himalayas. As noted in the previous chapter, other Victorian women accompanied husbands and friends in search of big game.

Few women, however, went through a metamorphosis such as that of Florence Dixie. Renowned as a hunter and adventurer, Dixie would eventually abandon the gun and fight for social equality. Born in 1857, she was a twin and the youngest of six children of Archibald William Douglas, the seventh Marquess of Queensbury. Young Florence was only three years old when her father accidently shot himself while cleaning a hunting gun. The widowed Caroline Douglas converted to Roman Catholicism, then fled to the Continent with her children to escape ostracism and legal issues. Florence lived in various locales during her childhood, learning to enjoy a variety of outdoor activities including shooting, riding, and swimming. By age ten, she had published her first poetry. A second blow, however, struck the family in 1865, when her older brother Francis died while trying to scale the Matterhorn.[2]

An active, vibrant woman, Florence married Sir Alexander Beaumont Churchill Dixie in 1875. The couple had two sons. Refusing to let motherhood restrict her desire for adventure, she and her husband began planning a shooting expedition to Patagonia in southern South America. Considered one of the more remote and unknown places in the world, and supposedly inhabited by cannibals, Patagonia's lure shocked family members and friends. Lady Dixie, however, had her own reasons for the journey:

> Palled for the moment with civilisation and its surroundings, I wanted escape somewhere where I might be as far removed from them as possible. Many of my readers have doubtless felt the dissatifaction with oneself, and everybody else, that comes over one at times in the midst of the pleasure of life; when one wearies of the shallow artificiality of modern existence; when what was once excitement has become so no longer, and a longing grows up within one to taste a more vigorous emotion than that afforded by the monotonous round of society's so-called "pleasures."[3]

To travel as easily and efficiently as possible, Dixie began paring the long list of supplies but still included two tents, a variety of cooking utensils, and a supply of food, not to mention two kegs of whiskey. Combined with their personal luggage and firearms, the goods required twelve horses to carry them.

While Patagonia lacked the dangerous game and hostile tribes of Africa, it presented its own difficulties. On one occasion, Dixie's hunting party was threatened as a fierce brush fire roared toward camp.[4] Indian guides quickly set counterfires in the grass. The effort proved successful as the main blaze swept harmlessly by, though the thick smoke left the hunters choking and the threat of sparks igniting their ammunition caused additional concern. A few days later, an earthquake struck the region. Dixie was jolted by the "heaving of the ground, resembling a sea-swell," that left her with a "sickly sensation of helplessness," she later wrote.[5] Aftershocks continued for several minutes.

After weeks of travel and camping in the wild, Dixie was forced to make the "shifts and expedients of camp life" Mssrs. Lord and Baines had written of a decade earlier. When Patagonian winds so pummeled her skin that her face was "swollen to an almost unrecognizable extent, and had assumed a deep purple hue, the phenomenon being accompanied by a sharp itching," she adapted by creating a makeshift mask from a blanket.[6] The Victorian niceties of bathing in a camp tub were forgotten when she discovered cold mountain water cascading into a clear pool. "I lost no time in undressing and indulging in the luxury of a plunge, which greatly refreshed and invigorated me after the long tiring day I had undergone," she noted.[7]

Dixie quickly learned that sidesaddle had to be abandoned when hunting the South American ostrich (rhea). Riding after the flightless birds required good equestrian skills and also demanded that when horses stumbled, riders had to roll with the fall. Being unhorsed during one chase, she recalled, was "by no means the least perilous part of the hunt and generally knocks the breath nigh clean out of one's body! I know that several which I got in this manner did so, and I am quite certain that had I not been riding on the cross saddle I should have been killed."[8]

Bagging wild game was the main reason for the Patagonian expedition. While stalking a diminutive species of Argentinien deer, Lady Dixie carried a light rook rifle designed to shoot crows and vermin. She fired both barrels and twice wounded an animal, but the small caliber of the gun proved ineffective. "I could not make out what was the matter with myself and my gun," an aggravated Dixie later wrote. Her companion fired his revolver, once more hitting the deer. A native guide finally put it out of its misery with his knife. A trophy-conscious Dixie made sure the hide was properly preserved for her.[9] While hunting guanacos, similar in appearance to llamas but of the camel family, she was startled to find a mature guanaco suddenly stepping into her path. Before she could unsling her rifle, the animal had bolted over a hill. Dixie realized she needed to be within 150 yards of the guanaco to be in effective range of her rook rifle. Carefully she approached the animal after it had stopped to watch her. "He allowed me to advance till within the required distance," she later wrote, "but then, to my disgust, just as I was preparing to fire, leisurely walked another thirty or forty yards before he stopped again, watching me the while, as it seemed with an amused look of impertinence."[10] Despite her best efforts, she could not get close enough for a proper shot. The thrill of the hunt, however, was captured in her memory.

Lady Dixie and her husband returned to England, where she published *Across Patagonia* (1880). She had enjoyed the isolation and rugged natural beauty of the region and immediately began planning an expedition to Alaska, crossing the Bering Strait to Siberia, then visiting and hunting with the Tuski people. Her theme of a desire to once more break from the swift pace of civilization was evident: "I had hoped to study the manners and customs of this Asiatic tribe, and find in the solitude of those wintry scenes the loneliness which at times it is so sweet to find."[11] But events were stirring in South Africa that would propel her in a different direction. A series of clashes between British forces and native Zulus had finally left the British victorious, though at loggerheads with Boer settlers in the Transvaal. When tensions exploded into the First Anglo-Boer War (1880–1881), she broke her plans to hunt in Alaska and Siberia to become a newpaper correspondent for the *Morning Post* to report the conflict in South Africa. With her husband in tow, she once more abandoned her family to seek adventure, armed not only with the pen of the reporter but with the rifle of the big game hunter as well.

Accompanied by several British officials, the intrepid Dixie rode across the South African landscape to report her observations of both older Zulu and current Boer battlefields. She found the lack of privacy confining. Upon reaching the Bushman's River, her male companions dashed to enjoy a refreshing plunge into the river while the dubious pleasures of a cold bath in a basin in her tent awaited her. She also continued wearing a long dress in the field and opted for riding sidesaddle after Victorian fashion. Once, when her party's mounts wandered off, Dixie attempted to retrieve them with the only remaining horse. Using a conventional saddle, she found she had little control of her steed.

When the horse suddenly stepped into an anteater hole, both horse and rider tumbled. Unable to roll properly, she was fortunate that she was merely bruised: "The ground was very hard, and though I broke no bones I gave myself a good shaking."[12]

As was the case in Patagonia, Dixie reveled in the hunt. When hunting blesbok, a species of South African antelope, she suddenly came across a herd of more than two hundred head. Slipping from her horse, she fired at the disappearing animals with her twelve-shot Winchester lever-action repeater but succeeded only in wounding one animal. While stalking hartebeest, she hid behind some boulders as the animals drew near. Over the next dozen minutes, she played cat-and-mouse with the animals, maneuvering to get a clean shot. When the hartebeest finally discovered her and successfully bounded away, a disconsolate Dixie was suddenly appeased when a hunting partner bagged the animal.

Almost constantly accompanied by her husband or British soldiers, Dixie longed for the solitude she had known in Patagonia. While crossing the Drakensberg Range, she decided to leave the cart she was traveling in and hike into the mountains. Finally reaching a high ledge, she found it covered in luxurious grasses framed by mountain ash trees. "It was a spot of extreme loveliness . . . ," she noted, "one of its greatest charms was its perfect solitude, its complete isolation from the vicinity of civilisation, from which its protective height will long separate it."[13]

After visiting various battlefields, observing mounds of spent cartridges and the graves of the fallen, Dixie and her party rode to the famous diamond town of Kimberley. She observed diamond mining before continuing on into Zululand, where she visited deposed King Cetewayo, later campaigning for his restoration.

While Lady Dixie might have been considered an unconventional woman by mainstream Victorian society in her pursuit of big game, she conformed to the strictures of fashion of the era. Upon returning to Cape Town after her adventures on the veldt, she refused to appear in her "travel-stained, well-worn habit," instead purchasing a length of serge and harking to the tailor of the local army regiment. She explained she wanted a short, tight skirt similar to a riding outfit. When her finished garment was delivered, she found it "tight and short with a vengeance!"

Almost scandalous for her day, the skirt did not reach her ankles. When she attempted to button it, the tightness wouldn't allow fastening across the knees. Dixie opted for a new design and different tailor, donating the "looking glass" dress to an admiring native woman.[14]

Dixie's nine months in South Africa were recounted in her second book, *In the Land of Misfortune* (1882). Though she went on subsequent hunts in the Canadian Rockies for bears, and in Arabia for gazelles, she apparently did not write memoirs of these activities.[15] Instead, her interests turned to social causes. In 1883 she championed Irish Home Rule, writing pamphlets and letters to raise money for evicted tenant farmers. So unpopular were her Irish efforts that she was attacked by a knife-wielding man dressed as a woman as she walked her dog one evening.

Lady Dixie's writing interests turned to penning novels and verse. The themes of sport and isolation of her earlier travels were replaced with issues of utopian societies, campaigns for sexual equality, and even advocating changes in women's fashions. She decried inequities in the workplace and singled out male dominance at universities. Women, she argued, had to control their bodies and, hence, population growth. In addition, she railed for changes in the divorce laws and in wedding ceremonies. Even the traditional line of succession to the British throne was challenged by Dixie. One novel, *Redeemed in Blood* (1889), was set in her familiar Patagonia but was filled with social commentary. In *Gloriana; or the Revolution of 1900* (1890), her female protagonist entered Parliament and helped engineer utopian reform. Other works portrayed women in heroic and reflective light.

Scandal and personal loss shadowed Florence Dixie. In 1883 her husband fell deeply in debt from betting at horse races, forcing the couple to move to smaller lodgings in London. In 1891, her twin brother James committed suicide. Another sister died in 1893. Her older brother's (Lord Queensbury) lengthy and infamous court struggle with novelist Oscar Wilde revealed the latter's homosexual relationships which eventually led to his imprisonment.

Hunting, once a passion, was not only abandoned, but became the focus of criticism in a pair of pamphlets Dixie penned: *The Horrors of Sport*

(1891) and *The Mercilessness of Sport* (1901). Both were re-published together as a revised edition by the Humanitarian League in 1905. "'Sport' is horrible," she wrote in *The Horrors of Sport*, continuing:

> I speak with the matured knowledge of one who has seen and taken part in numberless forms of sport in many and varied parts of the world. I can handle gun and rifle as well and efficiently as most "sporting folk," and few women, and not many men, have had experience of a tithe of the shooting and hunting in which I have been engaged both at home and during travels and expeditions in far-away lands. It is not, therefore, as a novice that I take up my pen to record why I, whom some have called a "female Nimrod," regard with absolute loathing and detestation any sort or kind or form of sport which in any way is produced by the suffering of animals.[16]

Reflecting on her experiences in Patagonia and South Africa, she admitted that she had hunted to please her companions or to collect specimens—"research of facts forced me to take part in many scenes from which my spirit recoiled."[17] In *The Mercilessness of Sport*, she advocated for substitutes for blood sports, including clay-pigeon shooting and whippet racing. "There are many amusements and healthy pastimes we could invent," she suggested, "in which horses and dogs could be utilized without taking life and shedding blood."[18]

While Dixie claims in these pamphlets to have revolted against hunting game while in South America and South Africa, her writings both in *Across Patagonia* and *In the Land of Misfortune* do not indicate her distaste enough to stop hunting. On the contrary, she is quite detailed in her descriptions of the chase, and she notes, "that the stalk is the only pleasurable and legitimate manner in which man can approach the wild denizens of any country, be it forest, prairie, or veldt . . . without that law in which skill is required, what true sportsman cares for the mere fact of killing?"[19] She alludes to an epiphany against blood sports sometime after she returned from her treks abroad. Stag hunting in the Scottish Highlands and participating in shooting driven pheasant with vast bags sometimes amounting to thousands of birds and small game in a single day, may have horrified her even as she was coping with changes in her lifestyle and her social-reform activities.

Florence Dixie's transformation from adventurous traveler and hunter to novelist and social activist undoubtedly confused and disturbed many of her contemporaries. When she died in 1905, *The [London] Times*, in its obituary, concluded that she would be best remembered as a "somewhat peculiar woman."[20]

NOTES

1. "Lady Florence Dixie in Glasgow" (Dundee: John Long, 1891), p. 9. Quoted in Catherine Stevenson, *Victorian Women Travel Writers in Africa*, p. 41.
2. Also see Marion Tinling, *Women into the Unknown* (New York: Greenwood, 1989); and Brian Roberts, *Ladies on the Veldt* (London: John Murray, 1965).
3. Lady Florence Dixie, *Across Patagonia* (New York: R. Worthington, 1881), pp.1–2.
4. Among the members of her hunting party was her brother John Sholto, the Marquess of Queensbury associated with the development of rules for boxing.
5. Dixie, *Across Patagonia*, p. 102.
6. Dixie, *Across Patagonia*, p. 60.
7. Dixie, *Across Patagonia*, p. 172.
8. Dixie, *Across Patagonia*, pp. 248–249.
9. Dixie, *Across Patagonia*, pp. 181–182.
10. Dixie, *Across Patagonia*, pp. 91–92.
11. Lady Florence Dixie, *In the Land of Misfortune* (London: Richard Bentley, 1882), p. 1.
12. Dixie, *In the Land of Misfortune*, p. 88.
13. Dixie, *In the Land of Misfortune*, p. 254.
14. Dixie, *In the Land of Misfortune*, pp. 413–414.
15. Jane Robinson, *Wayward Women* (Oxford: Oxford University Press, 1990), p. 66.
16. Lady Florence Dixie, *The Horrors of Sport* (London: A. C. Fifield, 1905), p. 5.
17. Dixie, *The Horrors of Sport*, p. 6.
18. Dixie, *The Horrors of Sport*, p. 23.
19. Dixie, *Land of Misfortune*, p. 137.
20. Quoted in Robinson, *Wayward Women*, p. 66.

FOUR

Edwardian Dianas in the Tropics

> "Oh! fellow sportsmen and explorers, beware of what you say and do in foreign lands, for whole nations and countries are judged by you, the first and possibly the only example they may have of your countrymen."[1]
>
> Catherine Minna Lady Jenkins, 1910

When Queen Victoria of England died in 1901, an era impacting much of the globe ended. Victoria, after all, had ruled the sprawling British Empire for more than six decades. Her son, the prince of Wales and duly crowned King Edward VII, was a renowned sportsman with a love for fast horses, fast yachts, and, occasionally, faster women. He also indulged in bird shooting and big game hunting in India. The Edwardian era, which spanned his relatively short rule, had one foot firmly planted in the haughty conservatism of the nineteenth century and the other stepping recklessly into a new century vibrant with optimism, opulence, and vast political and economic power.

Women travelers, and to a lesser extent big game hunters, had journeyed throughout the length and breadth of the world, finding few regions inaccessible. By the dawn of the twentieth century, the world had shrunk considerably. Travel books written by women were no longer sparse but had blossomed into hundreds if not thousands of volumes. Traveling women, including big game hunters, however, were still considered a novelty or unconventional by men. According to the male hierarchy of empire, women abroad had little effect on promoting imperialism. The colonies women traveled through seemed devoid of hostile natives, suggesting, as Sara Mills notes, those colonies were so under European control that women could travel without fear of sexual violence.[2] The view of indigenous peoples entertained by some women espoused a condescending or bigoted stance reflective of their perceived cultural superiority.

Women also had to straddle the fence, as Mills points out, between the intrepid fearlessness of imperialist actions (necessary when facing dangerous game or commanding native caravans) and the prescribed need to remain feminine and passive in their writings.[3] This duality led many women big game hunters to personify the game they encountered with tender metaphors of motherhood or cuddliness even as they leveled their rifles and squeezed the triggers. Interestingly, both Maria Aitken and Jane Robinson deplored the bloodletting, considering it distinctly unfeminine and revolting.[4] The slaying of animals, however, is intrinsic to that love of the chase described by José Ortega y Gassett. One simply couldn't have hunting without death. The opening of Africa, Asia, and other regions by imperialists exposed a seemingly limitless number of game animals—a resource to be harvested, or exploited, for whatever reasons. Conserving animal populations, while noted in various hunting books of the late Victorian and Edwardian eras and through the establishment of game laws and the creation of animal-preservation societies, did not become a central issue among European colonial holdings until after World War I.[5]

The early twentieth century provided all sorts of technological innovations to whisk travelers to their destinations with speed and alacrity. Steamships plied oceans in record time, while railroads cut land travel to a matter of hours or days. That same technology created efficient, modern rifles firing powerful, smokeless cartridges. New medicines allowed inoculation against or recovery from tropical diseases. A growing spirit of adventure propelled more women to take up the gun and embark on the shooting trail.

MARGUERITE ROBY

The call of adventure was particularly strong for Marguerite Roby. Abandoning her life of privilege in England in 1909, she decided to travel incognito as the maid "Henderson" to a wealthy woman and her children sailing for Australia. While aboard the steamship, Roby met a couple from Rhodesia (Zimbabwe), who suggested she visit Africa and try her hand at hunting. After reaching Australia and completing her duties as a maid, she embarked for South Africa, arriving in Cape Town, then traveling through Rhodesia for the Congo. Accompanied by a native youth named Thomas, Roby decided to tour the country by bicycle and shoot big game to boot.

Roby had tried to prepare for her African adventure. While posing as Henderson, she had attempted to find khaki cloth for a shooting outfit at various ports where her steamship had docked. She searched fruitlessly for a hunting outfit during stops throughout Australia and New Zealand, noting that in Sydney, Melbourne, and Auckland, for "an ordinary lady's shooting suit the tailors in these parts demanded a price which would have got me a magnificent ball dress in degenerate Europe, and my blood ran cold at the figures these gentry asked."[6] Roby finally purchased the khaki she desired in Samoa, then hired a Chinese tailor to produce her garments:

> In due course the suit turned up, and barring the fit and a few other drawbacks, it was all right. The breeches weren't exactly a Bond Street fit; they did not come up high enough behind, and the buttons were all put on upon the wrong side, so that the opening between buttons and buttonholes gaped forward. The gaiters, which I had told him particularly must button down the sides of the legs, buttons down the shin bone, and so if I had to creep on my hands and knees the buttons would of course hurt me. He therefore had another try, and by putting a fresh piece of stuff at the back of the pants made the wearer of these garments appear to be possessed of a tail![7]

Upon arriving in Johannesburg, she sought a local tailor to have a better-fitting shooting suit made. The tailor's measurements proved incorrect, so Roby personally brought the suit in for alterations. To the tailor's horror, she suddenly dropped her skirt and stood revealed in an old pair of shooting pants. From these he got the measurements, but the final product (which arrived while Roby was in Rhodesia) proved to be a better fit for a man six feet tall than for the diminutive woman. She eventually started wearing knickerbockers when riding her bicycle on jungle trails. When she met an English gentleman traveling with his wife, she noted their looks of dismay: "They looked quite shocked by my appearance—the knickerbockers were evidently too much for their sense of propriety—but I did not care, as I knew I looked clean!"[8]

The sweltering heat and humidity of the Belgian Congo (Zaire) caught Roby by surprise. During one trek, hordes of tsetse flies descended on the woman, their bites penetrating her gloves and puttees. On another occasion, a visiting trader helped crush flies that had worked their way under the veil of her jungle helmet and were biting her face. Fever stalked her throughout her entire journey. Though she took quinine supplemented with warm milk, and used alcohol freely, her delirious struggles frightened even her personal servants.

Roby's contact with natives revealed curiosity on their part but little interest in learning more of their culture on her part. She traded for food with local villagers, often by wearing her long hair down. On her first excursion to the village, she had been prepared to tuck her tresses up under her hat, but Thomas begged her not to: "No! Missisi leave hair down! All the women bringing tomatoes and fruit, and if Missisi leave hair down they want no payment. Leave hair down, much cheaper!"[9] Roby was sure many of the natives in the vicinity had never seen a white woman before. She likened her experience to one of a music hall dancer parading on the stage for all to see. In one town, a native woman not only admired Roby's hair and skin but proceeded to ask several embarrassing questions—of a sexual nature, no doubt. The Englishwoman preferred to ignore the queries.

It is difficult to determine Roby's experiences with firearms prior to arriving in Africa, and she may well have been a tyro. Her initial attempts at target practice were loudly criticized by a local white trader. When she finally hit the bull's-eye, she exclaimed delightedly that if she could hit such a small mark, then she ought to be able to hit most things. Though she could hit the target in practice, she admitted her first attempts at bagging game were less than successful. When she missed, her porters "would look at each other as much to say, 'She is no good!' whereas, later, when the animals began to get in the way of my bullets, their appreciation was as comforting as their former disapproval had been embarrassing."[10]

After weeks in the Congo jungles, Roby became proficient in the use of a Winchester Model 1895 lever-action rifle in .405, bagging numerous heads of antelope and elephants. It was buffalo, however, that terrified her the most. While stalking buffalo near Kassendi, images of being charged and gored flooded her brain. Several times during the hunt, she tried to raise her rifle, but her arms wouldn't obey. "I was petrified with funk!" she later admitted. Had no natives been present, she might well have considered abandoning the hunt, but she was unwilling to further damage their rather shaky faith in her shooting skills. Summoning her courage, she once more brought the rifle to her shoulder, and, as she recalled, "in a spasm of fearsome bravery, I took pot-luck with the sights and pulled the trigger, much as I imagine, a suicide does."[11] As the wounded buffalo charged, the woman evaded it with fancy footwork, then breathed a sigh of relief when it finally collapsed.

An amateur ornithologist, Roby attempted to bag various species of birds for her collection. While trekking through oozing swamps, she spied a species of crane that looked unfamiliar. With shotgun in hand, she tried to approach the bird while staying within the cover of tall marsh grass. Stepping on a large rock to take better aim, she was suddenly pitched into the mud. Her rock turned out to be the tail of an enormous crocodile, which took affront to the woman using it as a perch. Moments later her gun bearer deliberately knocked her into the mud, or "in another two seconds I should have walked straight into the jaws of [another] tremendous crocodile," she recalled.[12]

If her bearer had indeed saved her life, it was one of the few instances in which she spoke highly of most natives in the region. Roby's narrative, published in 1911 as *My Adventures in the Congo*, recounted episodes of threats and violence posed by native laborers or travelers. Yet in the literature of women as big game hunters, such threats were certainly rare. Women had to assume masculine roles in breaking tension and maintaining discipline among native porters, but physical violence toward a white woman was virtually unheard of. Advice in handling natives provided by Francis Galton in his *Art of Travel* (1872) reflected long-standing attitudes of white colonists and explorers: "If a savage does mischief, look on him as you would on a kicking mule, or a wild animal, whose nature is to be unruly and vicious, and keep your temper quite unruffled."[13] Margaret Tabor, commenting on nineteenth century missionary Mary Slessor, noted that white women would seem to be at a greater disadvantage than white men among native tribes, but the women's "very defenselessness often appears as a safeguard to women," whereas a man could be considered an enemy.[14] Assuming the dichotomous mantle of female hunter and male leadership styles, women such as Marguerite Roby were, on occasion, exposed to native backlash against both authority and femininity.

During one of her early bicycle tours of the Congo jungle, Roby was suddenly confronted by eight natives armed with spears. When she refused their demand for gifts, the natives made threatening gestures with their weapons. The leader of the group once more demanded presents. Roby shifted on her vehicle as if to comply, then quickly produced a revolver, which she leveled at the ringleader. She knew she had only six shots and worried that if the tribesmen attacked she would manage to fire only a couple of rounds before they overwhelmed her:

> Death seemed very close to me at that moment, and little incidents from my past life, away over in far-distant England, floated before my mind's eye, like pictures on a cinematograph film. From the time I nodded to the time when my fingers closed on the revolver handle could only have been a few seconds, but those seconds might have been hours, so many thoughts were hurrying through my brain in that little interval.[15]

The pistol's threat, however, was enough to discourage the natives and force them to retreat. A shaken Roby dismounted her bike and continued on the path.

Roby must have felt the threat of physical violence, or she simply adopted the attitude of European overlord in an African country when she took to carrying a chicotte, or short whip. The brutality of Belgian rule in the Congo was well known by the early twentieth century. A burgeoning rubber industry in the region led to the enslavement of many tribes with attendant torture and murder provided by Belgian officials. The short whip of hippopotamus hide became symbolic of Belgium's seemingly merciless rule. For an Englishwoman to have carried one would have equated her with the dominant Belgians.

From her manuscript, undoubtedly written with her own best interests in mind, there is little to deduce regarding Roby's leadership qualities. That she seemed to have constant problems with natives is evident, but how much could be blamed on any personal inadequacies is considerably less clear. While on one trek through the southern Congo, for instance, the leader, or *capito*, of Roby's porters suddenly sat down to smoke a cigarette, refusing to go on until he was ready. Roby threatened him with her gun and chicotte as the rest of the porters watched closely. She was sure she needed to set an immediate example or her entire column could rebel. Forcing the capito at revolver point to continue, Roby walked directly behind another rebellious native. When he suddenly threw down his bundle and leaped into the brush, she seized him by the cloth wound about his waist, only to have the garment come free in her hand, the naked man disappearing into the foliage. When she discovered two more porters had deserted, leaving their packages, including a case of beer, lying on the ground, she decided to have a beer and a cigarette until the rest of the column caught up. Over the next day, the rest of her porters fled while she sickened from fever. Her self-prescribed treatment consisted of liberal doses of champagne, quinine, and morphine. Eventually she recovered to continue, but with a new group of porters, the old group save for the capito, having fled. The incident had an impact on her:

> It were idle to deny that the natives of the Congo are a lazy and slovenly race . . . those supposedly downtrodden natives, whom we have all read about, are very different in the flesh, and they would have deserted me a hundred times during my trip . . . had I not carried a chicotte. To be too lenient with insubordinate natives in such circumstance would be simply inviting disaster.[16]

Leniency was hardly on Roby's mind as her expedition finally reached Lake Kivu. Attempting to reach the opposite side by raft, her new porters rowed toward the middle of the lake rather than the shore. When the *capito* swung toward her with his push pole, she fired her shotgun into the air as a warning. Realizing her danger as the rest of the porters glared menacingly, Roby reacted in desperation. Laying about with her chicotte, she managed to quell the rebellion and ordered the boat to shore. Further threats were required to force the porters to unload the craft.

Roby returned to England nearly a broken woman. Savage bouts of fever had ravaged her body. When she asked for a looking glass near the end of her journey, she recoiled in horror: "I not only looked like one risen from the dead, but over my left temple one lock of my hair had turned quite white!"[17] Traveling through Uganda toward the coast, she was suddenly stricken by temporary blindness, a result of her multiple bouts with fever. Several terror-filled days ensued: "Filled with impotent despair, I sat there, alone, in darkness, trying to realize the awful thing that had befallen me—knowing that *I was blind*!"[18] After she reached Port Florence, a doctor provided her with cocaine to relieve the pain, as well as doses of quinine. During her return voyage to England, Roby slowly recovered her vision. By the time she finally arrived in London, she had lost almost fifty pounds.

My Adventures in the Congo, Roby's only book, recounted her experiences and hardships with vigor, though at least one literary critic accused her of exaggerating, then blistered her (with some justification) for "flagrantly disregarding the canons of tropical travel in reckless exposure of fever, the tsetse fly, and noon-day heat, as well as the use of liquor."[19] She also openly disputed the reports that the Congo was the bloody scene of atrocities committed by Belgian officials. Her two long chapters as a Belgian apologist based on her six months in the country detracted from her personal narrative.

LADY JENKINS

As Marguerite Roby experienced the trials and tribulations of traveling and hunting accompanied only by natives, so too did Lady Jenkins. Born

Catherine Minna Kennedy in Sea Cow Lake, Natal, South Africa, in the early 1870s, she enjoyed numerous outdoor adventures on her father's sugar plantation. In 1892 she married Lawrence Hugh Jenkins, a prominent lawyer who accepted a position on the judge's bench in Calcutta in 1896, was knighted, and was soon promoted to chief justice of Bombay. Life in Africa and India undoubtedly whetted Lady Jenkins's appetite for big game hunting.

In December 1904, Jenkins embarked on a shooting trip to Somaliland. She was accompanied not only by several British officers and professional hunters but also by Antonia Williams, a Welsh baronet's daughter who was traveling on a tour of the world. Williams apparently had not known Jenkins previously, having met her only when she arrived in Bombay. Preferring her Kodak and notebooks to a rifle, Williams recorded her experiences and observations of the expedition in a journal, took 140 snapshots, and painted eighteen watercolors. She bound her journal entries, assorted letters, photographs, and artwork into an album titled "Recollections of Somaliland by Antonia Williams, 1904–1905."[20]

It is difficult to ascertain if the Somali hunt was the first for Lady Jenkins, as she performed poorly afield. Antonia Williams noted that the woman "arrayed herself in a very long, full, green dress, with plush, and gilt buttons, and a very smart hat" as she mounted her pony in pursuit of game.[21] When a panther carried off one of the party's sheep, Jenkins and another hunter tracked the feline, but she missed her shot while her companion connected with his. In another instance, she accidentally shot a goat tied as bait for a prowling leopard.

After they had spent a week on the trail, elephants were spotted, though Jenkins was not in camp at the moment to take part in the hunt. When she returned and found the shooting party had already gone afield, she furiously demanded to go alone after the elephants. Barely restrained by some of the Somalis in camp, "she went to her tent in hysterics," Williams noted.[22] In a second attempt to bag a panther, her bullet hit a tree as the cat bounded to safety.

Antonia Williams noted that she got along fine with Jenkins but admitted in her journal that she was "a most tiresome woman—always running unnecessary risks and increasing the danger to every one else very seriously."[23] In addition, Jenkins continuously argued with the male members of the group as to when and where to hunt. Williams also deemed Jenkins to be a bad shot. By the time the shooting party returned to the Somali coast in January 1905, several elephants, panthers, and various species of antelope had been collected. As for Lady Jenkins, according to Williams's journal, her bag consisted of an antbear, a gazelle, and a spotted hyena.

Jenkins returned to India, where she subsequently hunted tigers. Perhaps her poor performance in Africa taught her lessons in regards to marksmanship and patience. Her shikari in India netted her five tigers, though she apparently did not record her experiences of the trip in a diary or journal. By 1906 she was ready for her most physically demanding trek—into the highlands of Tibet.

Jenkins packed her familiar long skirts for her shooting expedition into Tibet. Upon reaching the city of Leh, her shikari asked to see her clothing, explaining that fur lining had to be added to her jackets and skirts. Within a few hours she was amazed to see her garments spread across the stalls of Leh as local peddlers sought to match fur to the cut of the cloth. When they had finally finished the alterations and additions, the woman was ready for the frigid temperatures of the high mountain valleys.

Armed with her favorite double rifles in .375 and .303 calibers, Jenkins realized that the natives who would act as guides and porters would watch her closely for signs of weakness. Nibra, her shikari, was afraid her hands were too small for rifles and her feet too small for the rocky trails they would march over. Nibra also worried over Jenkins's physical appearance, "looking like a town lady and not a shikari, and being horribly thin and weak," that she would not be able to maintain the pace in the rugged land.[24]

As the hunting party headed into the mountains, Jenkins knew she had to prove herself. On her first shooting attempt, she missed a trophy shapu, a species of mountain goat. When the herd did not bound off as expected, she redeemed herself in her guides' eyes by bagging the animal with her next shot:

> No one who has not experienced the long, trying and tiring stalks can realize the delight of success, and I was more than glad, for so much depends on the shikari's opinion of your shooting, as if they consider you a bad or unlucky shot, they will not give you nearly as many chances, or take the great and untiring pains they do, for one they trust not to disappoint them by a miss at the end of a long, perhaps cleverly-arranged stalk.[25]

The cruel winds and climatic extremes of the Himalayas stressed the endurance and perseverance of Jenkins and her natives. During the early stages of her journey, the frigid intensity of the mountain air caused her considerable pain as her lips and cheeks became chapped and cracked. Within a few days, all her cold cream had been used. She envied her bearded shikaris, then secretly rejoiced when she noted even those stalwarts suffering from wind and cold burn. Though she met two other English hunters at Leh, she ignored their cracked and swollen faces, as well as their implorations not to continue her trip. As her party continued to climb, her chapped lips were so painful that she could not stand the taste of salt. She fashioned a mask out of an old pair of gloves, then redid her hair in the Tibetan style of tight plaits after the wind had caused her loose tresses to painfully whip her chapped cheeks. By the time Jenkins returned to Leh after her shooting trip, a hand mirror left behind from her first visit revealed the punishment her face had taken. "My face was a deep and brilliant red, green tinting the whites of the eyes!" she recalled. "My lips and cheeks were all cracked and chapped, as well as sore and tender, and looked as awful as they felt."[26]

Jenkins soon learned of the vicissitudes of travel in the mountains. Though her shikaris warned her of wearing long skirts and riding sidesaddle, she credited both fashions with saving her life. As her steed zigzagged over particularly steep Tibetan hills, the pony suddenly tripped. With her skirt momentarily caught on the exaggerated pommel of the sidesaddle, she kept from plummeting down a sheer precipice. By throwing herself flat and off the saddle, she tumbled down the rocky slope opposite rather than over the ledge. Her porters scrambled to keep her from sliding into the abyss. "It took a long time for the men to get down to the pony and bring up the saddle, she recalled, "but I was glad to have more time to recover, for I shook and trembled dreadfully, and I did not want the men to see how unnerved I was. It was some days before I realized how magnificently and completely I was bruised."[27]

By the time she reached the Rupshu tableland at an altitude in excess of 15,000 feet, Jenkins was suffering from mountain sickness she described as a "terrible headache, and after every 20 minutes or half-hour's sleep a dreadful awakening, as struggling into an upright position imagining that you will die gasping for breath if remaining lying down."[28] Slowly, she adjusted to the altitude. When she spied three Ovis ammon, the great wild sheep of the mountains, she threw caution to the winds. The thought of bagging the elusive sheep with its magnificent curled horns left her heart pounding: "I wish I had words to describe my feelings then, after all those weary weeks of marching to be at last in sight of the animal I most wished to shoot, and the horrid dread that I should miss my chance!" Even as she sighted her rifle, the largest of the sheep suddenly became uneasy. With the animal silhouetted against the sky, she fired. Though the sheep dropped, it was up in an instant and dashing away. Scrambling nearly breathlessly along the precipices, Jenkins followed weak-kneed as the sheep disappeared beyond another ridge and toward a small glacier. "I sank down, absolutely done, and feeling very ill, my heart thumping, and a bursting feeling in my nose and ears," she later wrote. After a brief rest and a meal, she attempted to trail the wounded beast, but with poor results. "I have always held that no sportsman should leave a wounded animal, but circumstances, and these terrible altitudes, were too strong for me," she finally admitted. Happily for her, however, the shikaris found the Ovis ammon dead on the glacier and brought her the trophy head and a supply of mutton.[29]

Rather than give up her pursuit of trophies, Jenkins and her little band continued deeper into the mountains. Heavy snows enveloped her camp. During one frigid night, five sheep, two goats, and two ponies froze to death. Soon after, food became scarce. Huddled with her shikaris in her sodden tent, Jenkins seemed to become depressed as she remembered her "loneliness and misery might have been easier to bear if I had had an English-speaking companion or a book, and even if I had possessed a book it would have been too dark to read it, my last candle-end having been burnt more than a month before."[30] She developed frostbite in one foot, even though she wore fur boots and four pairs of socks, and recalled the incredible agony of hobbling about while trying to hunt. Succumbing to their misery, five of her porters deserted, but returned after realizing the woman was their best source for obtaining food. Later that day, Jenkins shot an antelope, quickly turning the porters' scowls into grins. A mountain tarn provided some fish. When her expedition finally descended into a valley containing a small Buddhist monastery, the stunted trees surrounding its wall were the first trees she had seen in weeks. "I was amazed to feel tears in my eyes," she admitted, "as I looked at those wretched examples of the trees and woods I love so well."[31]

After returning tired and worn to Leh, Jenkins recovered, then once more hefted her rifle for the journey back to Bombay, collecting additional mountain fauna including ibex and markhor. Upon returning to England, she penned *Sport and Travel in Both Tibets* (1910), a narrative taken from her notebooks describing only the initial shooting trip into the mountains. Her record did not indicate any of the tantrums or poor shooting as noted by Antonia Williams on the Somaliland trip but still revealed a cavalier attitude toward safety for herself and her porters in pressing into the mountains too late in the year and with too few supplies. Her book, however, emerged as a straightforward story of a successful hunt under often excruciatingly harsh climatic and topographical conditions—readers could challenge her wisdom but not her courage. Enhancing her text were more than two dozen colored plates from watercolors she had painted while on the trail. Her trophies were hung on the "dear old oakpanelled walls" at her home at Cilbronnau in Wales, then later in the Guildhall in Cardigan. Apparently she did little writing beyond her Tibetan title until the publication of a novel, *Through Hawsepipe to Cabin Door* (1924), a work of seafaring adventure. She remained in Wales until her death.

MRS. S. L. BAILLIE

Like Lady Jenkins, S. L. Baillie also enjoyed the pursuit of big game in India. The daughter of Mr. J. W. Smith of Oundle, Northants, in England, she was born in 1856, the year before the Great Mutiny would sweep through the Indian subcontinent. Her father taught her riding as a toddler, and her childhood was filled with traditional foxhunting. She married William W. Baillie, an Indian army chaplain, then accompanied him to his assignment in Bombay. Rather than be left behind in some military cantonment, she chose to participate with her husband and friends in hunts after big game. If Reverend Baillie was unable to go afield, she was not afraid to pursue game in the company of only a native shikari or two.

Mrs. Baillie immediately found India a literal beehive of insect activity. Once, while she was bird hunting with a female friend, a cloud of bees suddenly descended on her companion. Baillie bravely picked bees from the woman's hair, removed stings from her face, and then had to contend with the angry insects as they shifted attention to her. After one painful sting, she allowed the bees to crawl wherever they wanted. Eventually, the two women lay in the tall grass to alleviate their suffering until villagers appeared with bundles of dry grass and torches to drive the bees away.

To combat ticks in the jungle, Baillie invented a garment she dubbed "next to nothings."[32] Little more than an oblong bag with slits for leg bags and sleeves, the silk garment could be tied around the neck, wrists, and ankles. She liberally rubbed kerosene and tobacco juice at her neck and wrists, recalling their vile smell was a necessity to keep the ticks off. When returning from a shooting trip, she pulled off her "next to nothings" and found hundreds of ticks on the outer surface but unable to get inside. The garment was then dumped into a bucket of boiling water and readied for its next use.

After stalking buffalo through tropical swamps, Baillie discovered her socks covered with blood. Pulling off her gaiters and stockings, she found long, fat leeches attached to her feet. By using a combination of chewing tobacco and salt, she managed to rid herself of the bloodsuckers. She also found her shoes and bedding alive with scorpions. Once, while throwing a skirt over her head as she dressed, Baillie was stung by a scorpion hiding in the garment's folds. She found the arachnid, chopped it to a pulp, and then applied its remains to the wound as a poultice.

The discomforts of insect infestations notwithstanding, Mrs. Baillie took to the forests to hunt whenever possible. When she first arrived in India, she used a double-barrel .360 Express, which was considered too mild for larger game, particularly tigers. Ridding herself of the .360 on the advice of other hunters, she purchased a .500 Express black-powder rifle. Though considered obsolete even by early twentieth century standards, it weighed only a fraction over eight pounds and was quite manageable for her to shoot.

As with many women hunters, Baillie had to prove herself in the eyes of local game guides. After wounding a panther from her perch in a machan, she descended from the platform to follow the animal into a thick stand of bamboo. She motioned to her native beaters to stand ready with their axes and clubs. Not trusting the woman, the natives preferred staying well away from her as she entered the thicket. When she finally spotted the panther, she fired again but only wounded the animal. The panther "whipped round and snaked along the ground straight for me," she later recalled. "It was the matter of an instant. I never would have believed that a crippled animal could come at that pace: he was at my feet, practically on them, as I remember quite well running backwards two steps to avoid him before I got my aim. I fired the second barrel and he rolled over on his back." The gleeful beaters quickly clustered around her. "We will not be afraid of going out with the mem-sahib again," exclaimed their leader.[33]

Baillie's trust in her shikaris grew with familiarity and their trust in her shooting prowess. While hunting ibex, she worked her way uphill, then fired across a broad valley at a heavily horned ibex even though the beast was virtually covered by her sight bead. Her first shot sent the animal springing away, but she had time to fire twice more. Nibra, her shikari, suddenly noticed the ibex, undoubtedly wounded, standing still on a distant ledge. Fatigued and unable to climb any further, she handed her rifle to her shikari to finish the pursuit. As Nibra clambered upward, Baillie began a sliding, bruising descent down the mountainside. Her grass shoes disintegrated, and she was forced to continue her scramble downward in stocking feet. In the darkness of early evening, she finally reached the bottom, the soles of her feet bloody. Later, at camp, Nibra brought in the head and skin of the ibex—her long-distance shot had paid off. The ibex skin was eventually transformed into a carriage rug as a memento of her hunt.

In 1913 Mrs. Baillie faced her most serious encounter with India's wild game. While stalking bears in northern India, she and her shikaris spotted the paw of a bruin protruding from a cave. Unable to see the bear clearly, she handed her rifle to a shikari so she could climb on some rocks for a better look. At that critical moment, the bear charged from the cave and the shikaris scattered. "I was facing him," Baillie recalled, "and in an instant he had knocked me flat on my back, seized my thigh in his mouth and was shaking and worrying it as a terrier does a rat."[34] The bear suddenly lunged for her face, but its jaws snapped shut on her shikari helmet which had fallen over her eyes. As the shikaris regrouped and began yelling, the bear fled. The woman ordered one of the natives to retrieve her hat while she examined her damaged leg: "The teeth had gone through the fleshy part of my leg, rather deep, half-way between the knee and hip, missing the bone, and I poured water into the wounds from my drinking bottle to clean them out. Of course I lost a good deal of blood and felt rather faint again before I finished."[35] Her shikaris carried her to camp where she syringed the wounds with disinfectant. A native doctor dressed the deep gouges and watched for infection. Baillie convalesced for five weeks before returning to her tiger hunting haunts.

In 1914 Mrs. Baillie was treated with the singular honor of being the only woman represented among dozens of big game hunters featured in the folio-size *British Sports and Sportsmen: Big Game Hunting and Angling*.[36] She returned to London where, at age 65, she wrote her only book, *Days and Nights of Shikar* (1921). Adorning the book as a frontispiece was a watercolor she painted depicting the trophy tiger she had bagged.

GABRIELLE VASSAL

As with Mrs. Baillie, Gabrielle Vassal also accompanied a soldier husband to remote ports of call. For Mrs. Vassal, it was following her husband, a French army doctor, to his assignment in Annam (Vietnam). Born Gabrielle M. Candler in Uppingham, Rutland, in England, she was determined to help her spouse at the Pasteur Institute at Nha Trang. As she was about to depart the comforts of the English countryside, her English friends told her to welcome the adventure, while the couple's friends in Paris "bid us goodbye . . . and took leave as if they might never see us again," she recalled.[37] With a shiver of apprehension, the newlywed boarded her ship. At least, she noted with relief, their destination was not going to be Martinique or Timbuktu!

Working in southeast Asia combined adventures and physical hardship for Vassal. She would wake at 6 A.M., and bathe in the ocean before the sun became too hot. The pleasure of the bath, however, also carried a caveat: "Sharks only lend the necessary spice of excitement."[38] Further excitement was provided by the region's insect life as Vassal embarked on a shooting trip between Hanoi and Haiphong. Stepping from her boat, she proceeded to use a series of boulders as cover to sneak closer to her quarry. When she raised her rifle to her shoulder, she was suddenly stung on the eyelid by an ant. Within moments, she was being bitten fiercely all over. "Instinctively I threw my gun away and tore off my clothes without a moment's hesitation," she later noted. "Underneath my dress I was literally red with enormous red ants, which were doubling themselves up in order to penetrate my skin more deeply."[39] She donned a bathing dress she had in the boat while her other clothes were cleaned of the pests.

Nor were ants Vassal's only encounter with Vietnam's creatures. As she rode along a hunting trail, a seven-foot python suddenly slithered across her path. When her horse spooked, she dismounted, trying to jump as far away from the serpent as possible. Her feet slid on the wet grass, and she ended up on the ground between her horse's legs with the snake only a few feet distant. Retrieving her gun, she aimed at point-blank range and killed the python.

An avid amateur photographer, Vassal traded her Kodak for an eleven-millimeter Gras rifle when a tiger threatened a Mois village. Though her male companions were reluctant to allow her to stalk the tiger, she persisted. She spent an afternoon shooting snipe to get used to shouldering a gun quickly, then trekked through rice paddies and jungle to reach the area where a blind had been erected under a bridge. Vassal and her two male cohorts prepared for a night of watching. She admitted to muscle cramps as she crouched in the crowded blind but fought the pins and needles knowing that large movements might scare the tiger should it be about. When the big feline finally made its appearance, it emerged from the jungle only three yards from their cover. "His big head alone seemed to fill my whole horizon," Vassal noted. The threesome fired. When the smoke cleared, the tiger was no where in sight. Expecting that they had been waiting under the bridge for half the night or more, Vassal was surprised to find that little more than an hour had elapsed. Rather than trail the wounded tiger into the brush, the woman and her companions waited until sunrise. The tiger, as it turned out, had only been able to bound a few yards into the jungle before succumbing to its wounds.[40]

Gabrielle Vassal recounted her Southeast Asian experiences in her first book, *On and Off Duty in Annam* (1910). The work achieved a measure of respect from at least one literary critic, but not without mentioning the notion of unconventionality: "Madame Vassal writes with the particularity of observation which seems to be the peculiar gift of woman travellers."[41] When France and Germany went to war in 1914, she and her husband returned to Paris, where he was soon named Health Director of the 32nd Army Corps of the Rhineland. She spent time visiting the front lines and penned two more books: *Uncensored Letters from the Dardanelles* (1916) and *A Romance of the Western Front* (1918).

After the Great War, Vassal once more accompanied her husband, this time as tourists, first to Tonkin near the Vietnamese-Chinese border (which she described in *In and Around Yunnan Fou* [1922]), then to French Equatorial Africa, where he was named health director of that French colonial holding. She viewed most of the indigenous population of West Africa as "pitiful humanity" toward whom "one feels pity and also, unfortunately, repulsion and indifference."[42] The climate, she found, was similar to what she experienced in Indochina, with attendant miseries from the local insect life. Her encounter with jiggers left her disgusted. After having a native doctor remove one of the insects which had burrowed under her toenail, she noticed a small white blister on the inner edge of her little toe. The blister turned out to be a jigger egg sac ready to hatch. "No picking or itching had warned me," she later wrote, "and yet in a day or two I should have had this whole family of jiggers thriving under my skin."[43]

Unable to muster the humanitarian concerns needed to assist her husband, and forced to cope with tropical heat and insect life, she looked for ways to break the boredom of their routine at Brazzaville. Big game hunting proved to be just that ticket. Joining several French companions, she trekked near the Kouyou River, a tributary of the Congo. Sighting a herd of buffalo in the tall grass, the party began a cautious stalk of the dangerous bovines. When one bull suddenly caught human scent, the hunters opened fire. Vassal did not notice any of the animals drop until one of the native porters excitedly pointed to a wounded buffalo kicking hard as it struggled to its feet. She raised her rifle and pulled the trigger only to have the firing pin snap futilely on an empty chamber. She had forgotten to reload her single-shot Gras army rifle. Fortunately, one of her companions saw the danger and administered the *coup de grace*. When a second wounded buffalo was discovered, she quickly reloaded, ran to the site, and fired the fatal shot. She later admitted that she had been determined to prove her nerve had not been shaken.[44] She described her adventures in Africa in *Life in French Congo* (1925).

After their sojourn in Africa, the Vassals returned to France. War erupted in Europe when Nazi Germany invaded Poland in September 1939. Within a year, France had fallen to the Third Reich. Gabrielle Vassal became a member of the French resistance movement, helping arrange the escape of downed Allied airmen, for which she was recognized by both the American and British governments. After the war, she wrote articles and gave lectures concerning her experiences. Vassal died in 1959.

ETHEL YOUNGHUSBAND

In 1905, Ethel Younghusband followed her husband, a captain in the King's African Rifles, to his command in British East Africa (Kenya and Uganda). Her observations of colonial life contained various barbs, such as "some of the high officials suffer from a disease rather common in Africa as elsewhere: it takes the form of an enlargement of the head, which makes them unpleasant people to be near, or have much to do with."[45] Nor were her less than flattering descriptions limited to white officials—the natives were also viewed, but from a distinctly bigoted stance. Her "Swahili" porters were "not remarkable for their beauty, having generally broad noses with expanding nostrils and loose flabby lips; their hair, which the men keep shaved, would be woolly and curly if left uncut . . . Some of the young women have pleasing, jolly faces, usually full of laughter, but they become very ugly indeed when old."[46]

She also contended that everything the natives said was a lie, they were "immoral," and since they were descended from slaves, "they ought to make good servants, having learnt to obey." Later, in providing a local tribal chieftain with the gift of a necklace, she provided her own condescending observation: "He was delighted, but took it royally: one could not mistake that he was better bred than the other [natives] we came across—even in a native breeding tells, in face and feature and dignity of bearing."[47]

Like Gabrielle Vassal, Younghusband looked for adventure in the hunt. She joined her husband on several shooting expeditions into the Ugandan interior. On one occasion, when her husband's rifle was accidentally sent with another sportsman's safari, she was miffed: They had no cartridges for the Rigby-Mauser rifle that had been mistakenly packed for their trip. Her husband quickly appropriated her .303 sporting rifle while she was relegated to using a borrowed military rifle of considerable weight and doubtful accuracy.

On another safari, this time armed with her .303, Younghusband feared for her husband's safety as he stalked a pair of rhinoceroses. As she worked the action of her rifle, the gun jammed. She heard a shot, then saw the rhinos burst from the bush. Making sure her spouse was not in the line of fire, she shouldered her now unjammed rifle and fired a round. The lead beast suddenly turned toward her. She knelt and fired again, driving the rhinoceroses back into the brush. As she glanced around for her native gunbearer and porters, she found them all safely ensconced in nearby trees. "When the rhino charged our way," she later noted, "they thought discretion the better part and left me to my fate." Hoping to get a better view of the wounded animal, Younghusband also attempted to climb a tree, "but there were no branches for me on which to get foothold, and my wretched boots slipped down the trunk, leaving me dangling, just being held by the arms by several natives."[48] Fortunately for the woman, the rhino did not reappear at that moment. She dropped to the ground, then followed the blood spoor into the brush where the rhino was eventually bagged.

When Younghusband returned to England, she penned her only book, *Glimpses of East Africa and Zanzibar* (1910). It was a typical work of the period, combining history and hunting with observations of native life, but without attempting to understand the natives. As she noted in her preface, "To know something, however little, of the places, people and native tribes to which one is going and with whom one comes in contact must add greatly to the interest of travelling."[49] The book was met with condescending reviews. The critic for the *Saturday Review* wrote: "In the main she is just a delightful gossip about the life she led and the sport she enjoyed with her husband in Uganda."[50]

LUCIE MCMILLAN

While Vassal, Baillie, and Younghusband joined spouses at military outposts, Mrs. Lucie McMillan accompanied her husband on an exploration and shooting trip along the Blue Nile in 1905. The McMillans, of St. Louis, Missouri, and transplanted to London, embarked on their journey with several English and European friends and servants. Mrs. McMillan kept a journal of her experiences, as well as a photographic record.

Travel by stern-wheeler up the Nile combined the discomforts of heat and insects with tableaux of changing scenery and exotic wildlife. Lucie McMillan noted the monotony of the journey and the myriad of mosquitoes that descended upon their craft in the evening. Meals taken on deck were served under a specially constructed canopy of netting fitted with lights on the outside to draw the insects away. Even the netting, however, couldn't keep the tiny assassins at bay. Every fold of the netting, McMillan penned in her journal, contained insects by "cupfuls, and with every step they 'scrunched' under our feet—being nearly half an inch deep on the deck!"[51] Once the party landed and set up tents, baking winds swept their campsite. McMillan recalled dust piled an inch deep on the floor of her tent and all her clothing needing washing. "Hands, face and hair are unmentionable," she complained.[52]

Charles W. L. Bulpett, an English friend who accompanied the expedition, noted that some unnamed member of the group had dubbed Lucie McMillan "the Nuisance." Improperly aligned sights dogged the woman's attempts to bag a hartebeest. Assuming that it was simply the woman and not the gun, a male companion fired fourteen rounds from her rifle at the antelope without hitting it. When she eventually bagged her first antelope, she did so by resting the barrel of the rifle over her shikari's arm. "The Chief did everything but pull the trigger, which last I hope I did intelligently," she admitted.[53]

When the expedition returned to England, Charles Bulpett wrote an account of their travels in *A Picnic Party in Wildest Africa* (1907). Besides his own text, he included numerous excerpts from Lucie McMillan's journal. Interestingly, though her contribution to the book was considerable, she was not included as co-author but was recognized in Bulpett's preface. Her adventures were also noted in a privately printed book, *W. N. McMillan's Expeditions and Big Game Hunting in Southern Sudan, Abyssinia, & British East Africa* (1906), written by Burchard Jessen, a Norwegian engineer who was a member of the expedition. Jessen's narrative included descriptions of a frustrated Mrs. McMillan being forced to climb a tree when the hunting party encountered rhinoceroses. On a subsequent hunt, the woman badly wounded a lion, then determinedly waited until natives finally found the feline—dead. "It makes a man hold his breath with wonder and admiration for a lady possessed of such undaunted nerve and pluck as that displayed by Mrs. McMillan," Jessen penned.[54] Her lion was mounted by the London taxidermy firm of Rowland Ward and prominently displayed in the McMillan home.

The handful of Edwardian women who hunted and wrote of their experiences in the tropics represent a small fraction of the women who stalked big game but felt no urgency in capturing their sporting memoirs on paper. A number of women did indeed hunt big game animals, and even had their feats recorded in a series of record books published by the Rowland Ward firm, but did not write of their shooting trips. As late as the eighth edition of *Rowland Ward's Records of Big Game* (1922), such women as Lady Margaret Loder (Thomson's gazelle), Grizel Hamilton (eland), and Lady Frances Scott (Axis deer), to name a few, were listed along with the trophy specimens they had bagged. Likewise, W. S. Burke's *The Indian Field Shikar Book* (1908) noted in its section devoted to trophies, a twelve-foot tiger shot by Mrs. Laurie Johnson in the Jalpaiguri Duars of India.[55] As with Loder, Hamilton, and Scott, Johnson did not record her experiences.

Other women accompanied spouses on various sporting journeys but provide minimal information regarding their adventures with the rifle. Mrs. M. A. Handley, for instance, traveled through much of southern India with her husband, a government forestry officer. She alludes to big game hunting in *Roughing It in Southern India* (1911) but mentions little of her own experiences. The same can be said of Mrs. Arthur Colville and Edith Maturin, both of whom accompanied their spouses on travels across Portuguese East Africa (Mozambique) and to the Zambesi River, respectively. Mrs. Robert Meikle co-authored *After Big Game* (1917) with her husband, but outside of some bird shooting, she rarely participated in stalking East African fauna.[56] Sporting adventures are hinted at in these books, but either these women were not interested in sport or they downplayed their own participation, perhaps because they considered it unladylike.

When Edward VII died in 1910, an old, established era was drawing to a close. The Great Powers of Europe, locked in an arms race and a latticework of alliances, would reel under the death and destruction of World War I four years later. Emerging from that chaos was a world of crumbling imperialism and a map of Europe redrawn. Social changes, including women's suffrage, became prominent focal points in the 1920s. Women as big game hunters would enjoy greater opportunities for sport abroad and pen books recounting their experiences.

NOTES

1. Lady Jenkins, *Sport & Travel in Both Tibets* (London: Blades, East & Blades, [1910]), p. 3.

2. Sara Mills, *Discourses of Difference* (London: Routledge, 1991), p. 22.

3. Sara Mills, pp. 21–22.

4. Maria Aitken, *A Girdle Round the Earth* (London: Constable, 1987); Jane Robinson, *Wayward Women* (Oxford: Oxford University Press, 1990).

5. John M. Mackenzie, *The Empire of Nature* (Manchester: Manchester University Press, 1988), pp. 200–224.

6. Marguerite Roby, *My Adventures in the Congo* (London: Edward Arnold, 1911), p. 7.

7. Marguerite Roby, *My Adventures in the Congo*, pp. 7–8.

8. Marguerite Roby, *My Adventures in the Congo*, p. 250.

9. Marguerite Roby, *My Adventures in the Congo*, p. 43.

10. Marguerite Roby, *My Adventures in the Congo*, p. 25.

11. Marguerite Roby, *My Adventures in the Congo*, pp. 204–205.

12. Marguerite Roby, *My Adventures in the Congo*, p. 102.

13. Francis Galton, *The Art of Travel* (Harrisburg: Stackpole, 1971 [1872]), p. 308.

14. Quoted in Dea Birkett, *Spinsters Abroad* (New York: Basil Blackwell, 1989), pp. 134–135.

15. Roby, *Congo*, pp. 65–66.

16. Roby, *Congo*, p. 269.

17. Roby, *Congo*, p. 151.

18. Roby, *Congo*, p. 257.

19. Book review in *Dial* (52: June 1, 1912), p. 431.

20. Antonia Williams, "Recollections of Somaliland by Antonia Williams, 1904–1905." The scrapbook contained Williams's journal, letters from her to home, and additional letters from several members of the expedition. There are also photographs, watercolors, sketches, samples of flowers, elephant skin and hair, and maps of the region. The manuscript materials and ornamentation are in the Department of Special Collections, Kenneth Spencer Research Library, University of Kansas, Lawrence, Kansas. The manuscript was identified by Troy Bassett, Department of English, University of Kansas, and presented in a paper titled "A Dangerous Woman: The Representation of Big-Game Hunter Lady Jenkins in Antonia Williams' 'Recollections of Somaliland, 1904–1905.'" The paper was delivered at Writing the Journey: A Conference on American,

British and Anglophone Travel Writers and Writing, Philadelphia: University of Pennsylvania, June 10–13, 1999.

21. Williams, "Recollections," December 16, 1904.
22. Williams, "Recollections," December 23, 1904.
23. Williams, "Recollections," December 27, 1904.
24. Jenkins, *Tibets*, p. 2.
25. Jenkins, *Tibets*, p. 17.
26. Jenkins, *Tibets*, p. 23.
27. Jenkins, *Tibets*, p. 39.
28. Jenkins, *Tibets*, p. 17.
29. Jenkins, *Tibets*, pp. 33–35.
30. Jenkins, *Tibets*, p. 64.
31. Jenkins, *Tibets*, p. 78.
32. Mrs. W. W. Baillie, *Days and Nights of Shikar* (London: John Lane, 1921), p. 76.
33. Baillie, *Days and Nights of Shikar*, pp. 63–64.
34. Baillie, *Days and Nights of Shikar*, p. 204.
35. Baillie, *Days and Nights of Shikar*, p. 206.
36. The "Sportsman," *British Sports and Sportsmen. Big Game Hunting and Angling* (London: British Sports and Sportsmen, 1914), pp. 351–353. The article includes a photograph of her trophies.
37. Gabrielle M. Vassal, *On and Off Duty in Annam* (London: William Heinemann, 1910), p. 13. The French edition was published in Paris in 1912.
38. Gabrielle Vassal, *On and Off Duty in Annam*, pp. 49–50.
39. Gabrielle Vassal, *On and Off Duty in Annam*, p. 80.
40. Gabrielle Vassal, *On and Off Duty in Annam*, pp. 251–256.
41. Book review in *Athenaeum* (1: May 13, 1910), p. 637.
42. Gabrielle M. Vassal, *Life in French Congo* (London: T. Fisher Unwin, 1925), p. 35.
43. Gabrielle Vassal, *Life in French Congo*, p. 61.
44. Gabrielle Vassal, *Life in French Congo*, pp. 153–154.
45. Ethel Younghusband, *Glimpses of East Africa and Zanzibar* (London: John Long, 1910), p. 101.
46. Ethel Younghusband, *Glimpses of East Africa and Zanzibar*, p. 30.
47. Ethel Younghusband, *Glimpses of East Africa and Zanzibar*, p. 159.
48. Ethel Younghusband, *Glimpses of East Africa and Zanzibar*, pp. 169–170.
49. Ethel Younghusband, *Glimpses of East Africa and Zanzibar*, p. vi.
50. Book review in *Saturday Review* (109: June 15, 1910), p. 828.

51. C. W. L. Bulpett, *A Picnic Party in Wildest Africa* (London: Edward Arnold, 1907), p. 26.

52. C. W. L. Bulpett, *A Picnic Party in Wildest Africa*, p. 46.

53. C. W. L. Bulpett, *A Picnic Party in Wildest Africa*, p. 73.

54. B. H. Jessen, *W. N. McMillan's Expeditions and Big Game Hunting in the Southern Sudan, Abyssinia and British East Africa* (London: Marchant & Singer, 1906), p. 403.

55. J. G. Dollman & J. B. Burlace, eds., *Rowland Ward's Records of Big Game*, 8th edition (London: Rowland Ward, 1922); W. S. Burke, ed., *The Indian Field Shikar Book*, 4th edition (Calcutta: The Indian Field Office, 1908).

56. Mrs. M. A. Handley, *Roughing It in Southern India* (London: Edward Arnold, 1911); Mrs. Arthur Colville, *1,000 Miles in a Machilla* (London: Walter Scott, 1911); Mrs. Edith Maturin, *Adventures Beyond the Zambesi* (London: Eveleigh Nash, 1913); R. S. Meikle and M. E. Meikle, *After Big Game* (London: T. Werner Laurie, 1917).

FIVE

Agnes Herbert, the Penultimate Diana

> "My friend shudders at my slaying a rhinoceros, but manages to eat part of an unfortunate sheep immediately afterwards. I wonder if the good lady's words ring true. She may be right, and books on sport and adventure are only for men and boys, the sterner sex. If, therefore, you, reader o' mine, should regard all forms of taking life as unwomanly, read no more."[1]
>
> Agnes Herbert, 1909

Perhaps the most prolific of all women big game hunters was Agnes Herbert. Editor, novelist, travelogue writer, and big game hunter extraordinaire, she was born on the Isle of Man to James Bateman Thorpe and Helena (Agnes) Thorpe in the early 1870s. Privately tutored, as were many young women of well-to-do families, she developed a knowledge and love of Shakespeare that were evident via the epigraphs in many of her books. She also admitted to reading all manner of shooting books in her youth: "Hints to beginners on how to shoot, hints to beginners on how not to shoot; how to open your eyes; how to hold your rifle that you feel no recoil; how the rifle must be fitted to your shoulder or you cannot do any good at all with it; and (gem of all) how to be a good sportsman—as though one could learn that from books!"[2] Such shooting texts, she noted, were written by men for men, and their applications did not necessarily fit a woman. Herbert " 'chucked' all systems and manufactured rules" for her own shooting style, keeping both eyes open and bringing her guns to her shoulder as they fit her physique.

Herbert grew restless waiting for her hand to be taken in marriage. Rather than face what she considered the confines of domesticity, she and cousin Cecily Baird left the comforts of home for the rigors of early-twentieth-century mining camps in the Canadian Rockies. The women taught English-style cooking to Chinese kitchen workers and soon tried their hand at big game hunting. Herbert later noted "the charm of the chase captured us and we exchanged the gridiron for the gun."[3] It was an exchange that became a passion for more than a decade.

After their return to England, the cousins began to secretly plan a hunting trip to Africa. Afraid they would be laughed at as mere madcap women, the pair amassed a variety of stores needed for their journey. A benevolent uncle supplied them with a battery of heavy express rifles, fortuitously fitted with shortened stocks to fit his own short-armed physique. "My uncle selected [our guns] from his armory as being the ones of all others he would feel safest in sending out with us . . . his rifles might have been made for us," Herbert fondly recalled.[4] Included in the cousins' battery were three twelve-bore rifles, two double-barreled hammerless ejecting .500 express rifles, a .35 Winchester repeater, and a pair of twelve-bore double-barreled shikar pistols. Herbert's favorite rifle was her twelve-bore loaded with soft lead spherical bullets driven by 5½ drams of powder. Besides the guns were tents, medicines, boots, tools, and canned goods—all went into the larder. With bewildered family members at the docks to bid them adieu, the women began the first leg of their journey to Somaliland. "As to our courage," noted Agnes, "well, we could only trust we had sufficient to carry us through."[5]

Upon arriving at the port city of Aden after an uneventful voyage down the Red Sea in spring 1906, the cousins encountered immediate disapproval. The wife of a British officer warned them that "being women alone," they were "doomed to failure and the most awful things" and that a husband was an absolute necessity. Two officers on leave from India and about to embark on their own sporting trip into the Somali interior were afraid the cousins would try to join their safari. "They'll be duffers, of course," remarked one of the soldiers.[6]

Arriving at Berbera on the Somali coast, Herbert and Baird found that native vendors were not above gouging the women by selling equipment and stores at exorbitant prices. "I never felt the entire truth of the well known axiom, 'The woman pays,' so completely as on this trip," Herbert noted. "The women paid with a vengeance—twice as much as a man would have done."[7] Among the necessary items for the journey were forty-nine camels, a band of Somalis as porters and guides, and a Somali foreman dubbed "Clarence," who had served Herbert's uncle on one of his early safaris.

Venturing from Berbera toward the Golis Range in eastern Somaliland, Herbert felt she had to continuously prove herself to her native porters, who culturally viewed women as little more than chattel. When Clarence questioned her ability to shoot, she refused to put on a target-shooting demonstration, in which the vagaries of wind or blowing sand could affect her marksmanship and possibly deflate her image in Somali eyes. Rather, she answered simply that she'd had plenty of experience in England and Scotland and had been on other hunting trips as well. "My advice to any one who wants to be heard of is—Advertise, advertise, advertise," she observed. "If you begin by having a great opinion of yourself and talk about it long enough, you generally end by being great in the opinion of everyone else."[8] On her first stalk in the Somali brush country, she wounded an antelope but then successfully dropped the escaping animal with a well-placed shot. "Clarence's pleasure in my success was really genuine," she later wrote.[9]

Trekking through the Somali hinterland brought the cousins into contact with various tribal peoples. When she and cousin Cecily visited a Mijertain camp, Herbert was certain that the warriors never discovered the pair's sex: "Englishwomen were not exactly thick on the ground, and I think it possible [they] had never previously seen one" and probably thought how "particularly undersized, emasculated English sahibs these two were."[10] In general, the Englishwomen viewed the natives as primitive and thought "a visit to a Somali encampment makes you feel a trifle dirty."[11]

As the cousins marched farther into the interior, they began to leave the conventions of Edwardian fashion behind. "At first we elected to don a silly little skirt that came to the knee, rather like the ones you see on bathing suits, but we soon left the things off, or rather they left us, torn to pieces by the thorns," wrote Herbert in her notebook.[12] Trousers and khaki knickers soon supplanted the skirts. Coiffures, too, changed in the African bush. "Contrary to the accepted custom of lady travellers, we did not suffer the discomfort of wearing our hair in a plait down our backs," Herbert noted, after giving all of her hairpins to Somali women. "We 'did' our hair—mysterious rite—as usual. By the time I had finished . . . my golden hair was hanging down my back."[13] When going afield, however, their long tresses were pinned up under their shooting helmets. After several weeks of hard hunting, however, the cousins were no longer concerned with making a fashion statement. "Our clothes were now in a shocking state of repair, or disrepair," Herbert admitted. "What with wait-a-bit-thorns, drenching rain, torrid sun, wriggling on the ground, kneeling and grovelling about, we were the most awful scarecrows you ever saw. But we were intensely happy."[14]

Happy, perhaps, but other difficulties soon arose. Thunderstorms ravaged the area. Lightning struck Cecily's tent (she happened to be in Herbert's at the time), producing some startling results: "The lightning split the bamboo tentpole into shreds and threw splinters about that, when collected, made quite a big bundle. The hats and clothes which were hanging on to the pole were flung in all directions, but nothing was burnt."[15] The storms soaked all their belongings, including tents and bedding. To combat potential fever from the damp conditions and pesky mosquitoes, Herbert swallowed copious doses of quinine, while Baird preferred a tumbler of whiskey and water.

Cleanliness was also a concern for the women. After weeks of furtive and brief baths in their tents, the cousins were overjoyed when they discovered a small, secluded lake. To splash into the water without proper attire disturbed their Edwardian sensibilities. Using khaki-colored native robes, the women quickly fashioned rudimentary bathing suits that left their arms bare, arms that had not been exposed to weeks of hot Somali sun and wind. As Herbert observed, "from the wrist up our skin was as white as white could be, but from the wrist down we were Somali color to our fingertips." With the curious bearers and shikaris lined up to see them bathe, the women dashed into the water. "We dived, we raced, we floated, we dabbled, until at last we knew we must get out, for the water was quite cold," Herbert noted.[16] Though the khaki color washed from their ersatz suits, the nonplussed women enjoyed their dip. During the night, away from prying eyes, they once more entered the lake for a more thorough scrubbing.

The primary focus of the expedition was, however, to bag big game trophies. Upon reaching the Haud region, both Herbert and Baird marched into the rugged scrub brush after various types of antelopes. As Herbert revealed: "Much though I love the old primitive instinct of pursuing, I am not able to forgo the shot, and particularly when I want a lovely pair of horns."[17] With cool bravery, they faced charging lions. Herbert, nearly bowled over by one leaping feline and sent spinning into a thorn bush, was forced to use a hairpin to extricate a long thorn from her thigh. Later, when visiting the nearby camp of a Somali chieftain, the mullah questioned the women why they should be hunting lions instead of being married and tending to their husbands.

Native porters provided difficulties for Herbert as well. While chasing kudu, Herbert's gun bearer became entangled in some vines, accidentally firing the .500 express he was carrying. As this was a rifle with exposed hammers, he had to have been handling the gun with hammers at full cock—a dangerous habit to be sure. The bullet whizzed past Herbert's head and crashed through the underbrush. Trembling, she slumped, then angrily ordered the gun bearer back to camp. "It was very cowardly to be so upset," she wrote, "but I hate unknown and quite unforeseen dangers, and an unsuspected bullet at close quarters demoralizes me."[18]

Even the campsite produced problems. A Somali factotum dubbed the "Butler" not only deserted camp but also stole a camel, a supply of food, and Herbert's .35 Winchester rifle. Determined to find the miscreant, she saddled another camel, grabbed her .500 express rifle, and set out in pursuit. Hard riding on the camel upset her stomach, but she persevered. When the thief finally came in sight, he drove his camel toward a tangle of thorns and scrub brush in a final attempt to escape. Throwing her rifle to her shoulder, Herbert fired a warning shot that promptly brought the thief to a halt. Back at camp she threatened him with indictment for theft once the expedition returned to Berbera. The "Butler," who had previously worked for another white woman, begged forgiveness, explaining that his first employer always remained at home and his present job was confusing, as both Agnes and Cecily preferred to live in tents and hunt wild game. In another instance, when two Somali camel drivers took to settling an argument with spears, Herbert uncased her express rifle and threatened to shoot both combatants if necessary. Although the Somalis did not understand English, the woman's aggressive gestures and shrieks were enough to force them to desist with only slight bloodshed.

Herbert survived two animal attacks during the expedition. After downing a bull oryx, she and Cecily rode to the fallen antelope. Suddenly, the oryx regained its feet and attacked the dismounted Herbert. Thrusting with its rapier-like horns, the oryx stabbed the woman in the arm. Knocked to her knees, she watched her cousin shoot the beast before it could renew its attack. Back at camp, Cecily studied the suturing procedure from their medical book and proceeded to stitch Agnes's wound. In an encounter with a wounded lioness, the big cat sprang at Herbert even as Cecily fired at a range of less than six yards. The lioness, with a fatal and bloody wound to its head, managed to sink its claws into Herbert's leg as she fell backward. Half pinned under the dead lioness, Herbert sensed her cousin and the native shikaris gathering about, expecting the worst. Fortunately for her, only one of the claws had seriously gashed her thigh, a wound quickly cleansed with iodine and bandaged.

On many occasions, the cousins carried their shikar pistols in addition to their heavy rifles. Usually double barreled, though sometimes having four barrels superimposed in pairs, shikar pistols fired a solid bullet or shotshell. Used by hunters as an emergency weapon when facing dangerous game in ticklish situations, these pistols more closely resembled short-barreled, pistol-gripped versions of double rifles or shotguns.

Designed to deliver their projectiles at close range, shikar pistols were deadly. With excessive recoil transferred to the wrist and arm, shooters needed a strong, firm grip. Herbert was forced to wield her shikar pistol when an ard-wolf attacked her as she entered some brush: "A glare of green eyes and snarling teeth, a flat yellow head shot out as a snake strikes. My coat sleeve was gripped in a gin of white fangs, but only the incisors cut into my flesh—caught by the left arm in a flash. Before worse could happen I pulled my shikar pistol from my belt."[19] When the smoke cleared, the wolf, still gripping her sleeve, was dead. She made it a habit of keeping the pistol close to her cot during the night.

Despite the encounters with oryx, ard-wolf, and lions, Herbert faced her most perilous moment while stalking rhinoceroses in heavy thorn brush. Accompanied by Clarence and another Somali nicknamed "the Baron," she fired at a partially hidden rhino, even though her common sense told her it was a difficult shot. The wounded beast charged:

> I fired again, another shoulder shot. This bullet "told" heavily, and the maddened creature, smarting and furious, passed me like the wind and charged like a Juggernaut right over the Baron, who, in meaning to evade the rush, fell into it through the unexpected agility of the brute. A most awful stifled shriek arose as my poor fellow went down. Frightened as I was, I felt I should be everlastingly branded to myself as a coward if I made no attempt to save the man, although I understood how altogether impossible salvation was just then.[20]

Though the rhinoceros was killed, so was the Baron. Upon returning to camp, Herbert threw herself onto her cot, blaming herself for the Somali's death. "It does a woman good to cry, so I wept and wept," she admitted.[21]

As their expedition drew to a close, the women were visited by the two British officers they had earlier met in Berbera. The officers, dubbed "the Leader of the Opposition" and "Ralph" by Agnes, had also enjoyed a satisfactory hunt. The cousins displayed their trophies with pride, noting that theirs were more numerous and splendid than those of the opposition. Agnes also found Cecily spending more and more time with Ralph.

Upon reaching Berbera, the trophies were carefully packed aboard ship for the long voyage back to London. After returning home, Herbert began writing her account of the expedition. Published by John Lane in 1908, the book was titled *Two Dianas in Somaliland, the Record of a Shooting Trip*. For the most part, press opinions crowed their appreciation of the work. "This is a book to read, if only for its delightfully unconventional vein," noted *The Birmingham Post.*[22] *The New York Times* considered the adventures to be "realistic" and "fascinating" but also "heartless."[23] Negative criticism was evident as well. "Miss Herbert, judging by her trophies, is readier with the gun than the pen," sneered the critic for the *Saturday Review.*[24] Unconventionality was the focus provided by *The Spectator*: "The tone of bravado and devil-may-careness is irksome at first, when it is only a few simple conventions which the Dianas are defying. . . . When it comes to lions and rhinos and every known discomfort, we are captivated in spite of ourselves."[25]

Agnes Herbert, however, was not ready to consign herself to the role of spinster whiling away her time in the British Isles. Within a year of returning from Somaliland, she and Cecily began to plan a new expedition, this one in Alaska. After landing in New York City, the cousins headed by rail for Butte City (Butte), Montana, at Cecily's urging. A mining center, Butte was dubbed by Agnes "the ugliest town in all America."[26] It became readily apparent why Cecily had requested the special train to Butte—a rendezvous with Ralph Windus (the Ralph introduced in *Two Dianas in Somaliland*) had been arranged. Ralph, accompanied by the Leader of the Opposition, had recently completed a hunting trip in the Rocky Mountains. The expedition to Alaska was to be a foursome.

For the Alaskan jaunt, Herbert and her cousin eschewed the large-caliber double rifles of their earlier African hunt for smaller-caliber repeaters, even though they would face the likes of Alaskan brown bears. As Agnes recorded: "Since our Somaliland trip my cousin and I had transferred some of our affections—being women, and therefore changeable—from weapons of otherdays, and now meant to use as our main stand-bys a couple of small-bore magazine rifles, a .375 bore, and a .256 Mannlicher."[27]

In April 1908, the shooting party arrived at Kodiak Island. Traveling by native sealskin boats, or *bidarkas*, the group paddled up numerous rivers in search of game. Agnes was quite taken with the natural beauties of the region but had little good to say of the Inuits, Aleuts, and other natives living there. Reflecting the racist attitudes and English superiority of her day, she noted:

> Time and experience have taught Englishmen throughout the world that the only successful way to rule natives is by firmness tempered with justice, compelling them to feel a certain dependency upon their white associates. Beneath the skin of a native lies the heart of one born to be ruled by a superior hand whether it be that of his own kind or that of an alien race. Kindness is too often interpreted by them as a form of weakness, familiarity breeds contempt, and equality between the white and colored races will eventually end in disaster.[28]

For her, the Aleut village offered only "a terrible smell arising from the offal, carelessly thrown in heaps near the dwellings," an odor "so overpowering that the average white man is glad to escape as soon as possible from a visit to one of these camps."[29]

As in Somaliland, the cousins had to assure native guides that they were indeed experienced hunters. Facing an enraged brown bear that had reared on its hind legs, the pair dropped it with well-aimed shots. When Ned, one of their Inuit guides, followed the sound of their shots to the downed bruin, he was quite impressed: "You shoot all right, you bet." Herbert recognized the importance of the women proving themselves with a rifle:

> We had known from the very first that our men regarded the feminine part of our expedition very much in the light of an American dime show—a great deal of fuss and palaver, and very little when you really get to it. We did not mind . . . Why talk to them of [our] experiences—days with rhino, lion, leopard . . . it always seems to me that when anything you have done in the past looms very large and splendid in your eyes, it argues that you have not accomplished much today. Deeds, not words, count with natives.[30]

As the hunt continued, however, the guides slowly changed their minds as the women collected caribou, walrus, moose, and wild sheep.

The dangers faced by the cousins and their companions seemed less treacherous than those the women had met in Somaliland. In one instance, a wounded lynx attacked Cecily and was finally dispatched by Herbert, who clubbed it to death as its jaws ground through Cecily's gaiters. In another episode, a Kodiak bear reared threateningly on its hind legs after being shot before finally succumbing.

While sexual assault apparently had not been a danger on the Somaliland expedition, the wilderness of Alaska held new surprises. When an Inuit guide suddenly entered Herbert's tent and sat down next to her, the woman reacted with more than a veiled threat. "He commenced to say something, but words died in his throat as I ordered him out" she later recalled. "My fingers had jumped to my belt, and half instinctively I had pulled my shikar pistol out. I frightened my man all right. Familiarities were off henceforward . . . The management of natives in any country is always a difficult affair for women to tackle."[31]

During the Alaskan trip, the hunting party divided into two pairs. Cecily spent more time afield with Ralph Windus, while Agnes found herself in the company of the still unnamed "Leader." Cecily and Ralph had fallen in love and, upon the expedition's return to Seattle, were married. Herbert worried that the couple's infatuation during the hunt was too premature to lead to marriage: "One of the saddest things in life is that love is destructible."[32] Her own feelings, or lack of feelings, toward the Leader were seemingly hidden throughout the hunting trip until the very end, when he appeared in front of her after the wedding ceremony. "His eyes were smiling, smiling. Perhaps . . . I'm not so very lonely after all," she coyly admitted.[33]

After her cousin's nuptials and the brief festivities that followed, Agnes Herbert returned to England. During the next several months, she penned *Two Dianas in Alaska*, a work that featured several chapters by the Leader. Published by John Lane in 1909, the book was dedicated to newlyweds Cecily and Ralph Windus.

After the Alaskan adventure, Herbert apparently settled into the lifestyle of an author. With her favorite rifles cleaned and safely stored, she took up the pen to write *The Isle of Man*, an illustrated travel book published by Adam and Charles Black. Appearing in 1909, the book reflected Herbert's love of the island and her intimate knowledge of its peoples, myths and terrain. In 1911 she wrote *The Life of a Lion*, a juvenile fiction work based on her experiences with lions while hunting in Somaliland, complete with the familiar Shakespearean epigraphs.

Herbert, however, was soon planning another sporting expedition, this time to the Caucasus Mountains of the Russian Empire. The Caucasus of the early twentieth century were still virtually unknown to the outside world. A mid-nineteenth century rebellion by Murid tribesmen led by Schamyl against the czar's army had sparked the imagination. A few travel and mountaineering books described the region, while noted sportsmen such as Clive Phillipps-Wolley and Elim Demidoff, had also penned their big game hunting experiences in the Caucasus.[34]

Accompanying Herbert on this trip were her favorite shooting partner, Cousin Cecily Windus, though unaccompanied by her husband, and Cecily's brother, Colonel Kenneth Baird, an amateur anthropologist. She noted that Cecily had more difficulty in arranging for this trek. "That is the worst of being married. It has such tying ties," a disgruntled Herbert wrote.[35] With few ties binding her to home, the journey and adventure were of greatest importance. The tools of the hunt had become her new family: "The rifles of a hunter are like his own children, nobody else has anything approaching them. They stand on a plane apart."[36] Of the "Leader" of past hunting trips, there was no further mention.

Russian customs laws almost doomed the expedition from the start. Sportsmen could bring their firearms into the Caucasus, but cartridges were considered prohibited merchandise. It was undoubtedly hoped by customs officials that visitors would be forced to purchase Russian rifles and cartridges at exorbitant fees. The trio of Anglo hunters circumvented the laws in an inventive fashion. The women stitched little pockets into their underskirts, then crammed the pockets full of cartridges. "The drag and weight was terrific," noted Herbert, "and they stuck out like crinolines, besides barking our shins. Had anyone knocked against us—!" Baird, in the meantime, tucked his cartridges into a bandoleer and tightened it around his waist, covering the belt with his sweater and coat. Neither Herbert nor Windus chose to emulate his method: "I draw the line at a waist over twenty-four inches, and so does Cecily," Agnes wryly penned in her journal.[37] The hunting party made it through customs with their smuggled ammunition without a search.

Traveling by rail to Tiflis (Tbilisi), then to the rugged shooting grounds of Daghestan, Herbert described the region as "grey rocky walls [rising] to the sky, and about the lofty summits snow-clouds circle like the crowns of throned kings."[38] The sporting intention of the trio was to collect trophy heads of tur—the Caucasian ibex, a wild goat with massive, back-sweeping horns—as well as other game.

The shooting party made the acquaintance of a pair of Russian sportsmen who invited them to join in their hunt. Not wishing to offend them, Herbert agreed, though she observed the Russian officers "regarded Cecily's and my sporting predilections with ill-conceived amusement. I am so very used to that, and it has ceased to trouble me." But trouble her it did. She continued in her notes: "I don't know why a woman should be considered on sight to be unable to shoot as straight as a man, or stalk so well, or play the game, or understand the ways of jungly creatures. But she isn't . . . my Russian . . . had only unnecessary doubts of me and admiration for my rifle."[39]

The Russian sportsman accompanying Herbert quickly learned of the woman's shooting prowess. The pair stalked a small group of tur, with a difficult shot needed to bag a trophy animal from under a jutting rock shelf. Motioning her companion to grab her waist (Herbert didn't speak Russian), she leaned over the precipice, took aim at the quarry, and fired her Mannlicher twice. After tracking the wounded ibex, a joyful Herbert finally discovered the carcass on a snow-covered ridge. Her Edwardian morals were suddenly shaken when she found the Russian "very delighted also, for he rested congratulatory hands on my shoulders and looked so affectionately proud of me that I thought it wiser to damp his enthusiasm a little by suggesting his carrying home the prize. . . . This certainly drove all others out of my friend's head."[40]

From Daghestan, the cousins returned to Tiflis, with Kenneth debarking on an anthropological study of the region. The women continued by rail, then post road into Georgia to stalk the area near the Kouban

River. Invited by a local prince to hunt on his grounds, Agnes and Cecily trekked through thick forests after ollen, a heavy-antlered species of red deer. The going was difficult amid treacherous slopes, fallen timber and tangled willow skeins. "Stalking in the Kouban is a stiffish job," recalled Herbert in her diary, "and the hunter deserves all and more than he gets."[41]

Venturing into a bear's cave almost proved the undoing of the cousins. They had trailed the bruin into the fissure but recognized the dangers inherent in entering. "In a cave of winds like this in which it was difficult to hear, and impossible to see into corners, the game was too much to the enemy," Herbert recalled. As her eyes adjusted to the dim light, she discerned "two little glow-worm lights" as the bear watched them, admitting that "it was an eerie sensation, and my spine just pricked with a sensation as of pins and needles as I stood ready for anything and expecting Heaven knows what."[42] The woman threw her rifle to her shoulder as the bear charged toward the opening. Her shot dropped the animal, but in an instant it renewed its efforts toward her. Cecily finally delivered the fatal round.

As their shooting trip neared its end, an unforeseen difficulty emerged. Their host, the local prince, had fallen in love with Cecily. It was quite all right for Herbert to return to England, according to the prince, but her cousin would have to remain behind. When she reminded him that Cecily was married, the prince refused to accept that issue: "In my country a husband does not allow his wife to travel alone."[43] Deciding to leave secretly, the cousins departed from the prince's castle during the night. Though they traveled quickly, the prince appeared on the trail ahead of them. Embarrassed by his demand for Cecily to remain with him, he apologized profusely, re-extending the invitation to continue the hunt. Accepting his apology, the women calmly declined and continued their journey to Tiflis.

For Herbert, the trip to the Caucasus was the last of her grand sporting adventures. Upon her return to Britain, she wrote the third of her trilogy of big game hunting books: *Casuals in the Caucasus, the Diary of a Sporting Holiday* (1912). More travelogue than sporting work, it received only lukewarm reviews. "The feminine touch is at times too apparent, but the book remains wholesome, interesting and attractive to the reader of lighter books," wrote the reviewer for *Booklist*.[44]

After returning from Russia, Herbert married Commander A. T. Stewart of the Royal Navy and settled into a career of writing and editing. Recalling her shooting trips to Alaska and Somaliland, she wrote two more juvenile fiction works, *The Moose* in 1913, and *The Elephant* in 1916. From 1922 to 1929, she was editor of the *Writer's and Artist's Year Book* and also served on a number of literary councils in Great Britain. She penned travel books on Northumberland (1923) and Korea (1924), as well as numerous short stories, articles, and a novel written under a pseudonym. In 1931 she received the prestigious Officer of the British Empire award.

Herbert's writing career was not without some controversy. In 1930 John C. Phillips, a noted outdoors writer and the associate curator of birds at Harvard University's Museum of Comparative Zoology, published his seminal *American Game Manuals and Birds* (later retitled *Bibliography of American Sporting Books*). The compilation, largely based on the extensive personal collection of explorer and big game hunter Charles Sheldon, consisted of thousands of titles related to sport in North America. Under the listing for Herbert's *Two Dianas in Alaska*, Phillips included a decidedly accusatory annotation: "This book is fiction. Captain Radclyffe, author of *Big-Game Shooting in Alaska*, dictated most of the narrative."[45] C. R. E. Radclyffe's *Big-Game Shooting in Alaska* was published in London by Rowland Ward in 1904.

Phillips made no note as to why he considered Herbert's book to be fictitious, or that Radclyffe had dictated it. If Sheldon had offered the notion, that record is still undetected. Yet there are similarities between Herbert's and Radclyffe's books. Two of the photographs appearing in Radclyffe's, one of bear skinning and the other of a slain moose, appear in Herbert's book.[46] The photograph of the moose in particular reveals the photo was doctored to remove Radclyffe from the scene. As to why Radclyffe's photographs were printed in Herbert's work, one can only surmise that her camera was either not available or not working during those segments of her hunt and he simply lent the pictures to her. The pair may have been acquaintances, or even friends. Interestingly, the studio portrait of a fur-swathed "Leader" appearing in Herbert's book bears a striking resemblance to the image of Radclyffe appearing as the frontispiece in his work.[47] In addition, both Herbert and Radclyffe hunted in Somaliland, though there is no evidence that their trips coincided.

Of the two Alaskan trips, Radclyffe's and Herbert's, the former spent little time observing or describing village life, an issue Herbert included in her book. Nor did Radclyffe hunt walrus, though Herbert experienced a fair amount of walrus hunting complete with accompanying photographs. Herbert's narrative also includes the adventures of her cousin Cecily and Ralph Windus.

While the Phillips bibliography remains a monumental reference work, it has a number of flaws, particularly in the annotations. Phillips's listing for Alonzo Hepburn's *The Story of an Outing*, for instance, notes that it was "mostly about India," whereas the book is clearly about Hepburn's African safari with no mention of setting foot in India.[48] Likewise, his annotation for Mrs. St. Maur's *Impressions of a Tenderfoot* states that it contains "a great deal on shooting in Canada and West," while there is actually very little shooting content with Algernon St. Maur tramping about after game but rarely having a chance to fire his rifle.[49]

The dissimilarities in writing styles between Herbert's *Two Dianas in Alaska* and Radclyffe's *Big-Game Shooting in Alaska* certainly provide little allowance for Phillips's assertion of fiction and dictation. His annotation mentions nothing of the chapters attributed to the "Leader." Unless more information on Radclyffe, other than a few photographs apparently lent to Herbert, is revealed to prove her Alaskan book a fraud, it remains a singularly adventurous work penned by a prominent woman big game hunter.

More recently, Maria Aitken in *A Girdle Around the Earth* (1987) suggests that Agnes Herbert did not write *Two Dianas in Somaliland*, and that it may have been penned by a man.[50] Her case is based largely on the assumption that none of the photographs provided in the volume depict either Herbert or Cecily with the game they had bagged, hence the photographs may not be authentic. She also assumes that the writing style, "so brimming with 'Little Woman' asides," was probably the work of a man.[51]

In studying dozens of books written by men who hunted big game, photographs showing hunters and trophies are relegated to only a handful. Then there are the numerous volumes recounting big game hunts at which cameras were not present but were vividly illustrated by artists who created their drawings based solely on the text materials. Such illustrations also appeared in the works of Isabel Savory, Nora Gardner, and Mrs. R. H. Tyacke. Herbert's narratives should not be discounted due to a lack of posed photographs.

As for Aitken's contention that Agnes Herbert may have been a man, the record of her existence is indisputable. Of the dozens of reviews of *Two Dianas in Somaliland*, none allude to either ghostwriting by a man or a fictional author. As the book went through three editions, it is unlikely that it would have remained popular had the reading public been duped. Certainly her other books would have been rejected as well. In addition, a brief biography of Herbert is listed in various editions of *Who Was Who*.[52]

Herbert remained active in the British literary community for the remainder of her life. Apparently she remained close to her cousin Cecily, but the adventures of the "Two Dianas" ended prior to World War I, and there is no evidence suggesting she maintained an interest in big game hunting in her later years. Agnes Herbert died in 1960.

NOTES

1. Agnes Herbert and a Shikari, *Two Dianas in Alaska* (London: John Lane, 1909), p. 1.
2. Agnes Herbert, *Two Dianas in Somaliland* (London: John Lane, 1907), pp. 185–186.
3. Agnes Herbert, *Two Dianas in Somaliland*, p. 2.
4. Agnes Herbert, *Two Dianas in Somaliland*, p. 4.
5. Agnes Herbert, *Two Dianas in Somaliland*, p. 2.
6. Agnes Herbert, *Two Dianas in Somaliland*, p. 17.
7. Agnes Herbert, *Two Dianas in Somaliland*, p. 20.
8. Agnes Herbert, *Two Dianas in Somaliland*, p. 33.
9. Agnes Herbert, *Two Dianas in Somaliland*, p. 42.

10. Agnes Herbert, *Two Dianas in Somaliland*, p. 189.
11. Agnes Herbert, *Two Dianas in Somaliland*, p. 57.
12. Agnes Herbert, *Two Dianas in Somaliland*, p. 38.
13. Agnes Herbert, *Two Dianas in Somaliland*, p. 53.
14. Agnes Herbert, *Two Dianas in Somaliland*, p. 111.
15. Agnes Herbert, *Two Dianas in Somaliland*, p. 47.
16. Agnes Herbert, *Two Dianas in Somaliland*, pp. 208–209.
17. Agnes Herbert, *Two Dianas in Somaliland*, p. 97.
18. Agnes Herbert, *Two Dianas in Somaliland*, pp. 241–242.
19. Agnes Herbert, *Two Dianas in Somaliland*, p. 101.
20. Agnes Herbert, *Two Dianas in Somaliland*, pp. 130–131.
21. Agnes Herbert, *Two Dianas in Somaliland*, p. 133.
22. Book review in the *Birmingham Post*, quoted in Herbert's, *Two Dianas in Alaska*, "press reviews," p. 3. There are numerous other quotes from reviews noted.
23. Book review in *The New York Times*, Vol. 12, Nov. 9, 1907, p. 720.
24. Book review in the *Saturday Review*, Vol. 104, Nov. 9, 1907, p. 582.
25. Book review in *The Spectator*, Vol. 99 (Supplement), Nov. 16, 1907, p. 749.
26. Herbert, *Two Dianas in Alaska*, p. 7.
27. Herbert, *Two Dianas in Alaska*, p. 16.
28. Herbert, *Two Dianas in Alaska*, p. 89.
29. Herbert, *Two Dianas in Alaska*, p. 92.
30. Herbert, *Two Dianas in Alaska*, p. 66.
31. Herbert, *Two Dianas in Alaska*, p. 232.
32. Herbert, *Two Dianas in Alaska*, p. 257.
33. Herbert, *Two Dianas in Alaska*, p. 316.
34. Clive Phillipps-Wolley (1854–1918) wrote two works on hunting in the Caucasus: *Sport in the Crimea and Caucasus* (London: Richard Bentley, 1881) and *Savage Svânetia* (London: Richard Bentley, 1883). Demidoff's book was *Hunting Trips in the Caucasus* (London: Rowland Ward, 1898). Both authors also contributed articles to a variety of sports encyclopedias and anthologies published in the era.
35. Agnes Herbert, *Casuals in the Caucasus* (London: John Lane, 1912), p. 6.
36. Agnes Herbert, *Casuals in the Caucasus*, p. 7.
37. Agnes Herbert, *Casuals in the Caucasus*, p. 9.
38. Agnes Herbert, *Casuals in the Caucasus*, p. 131.

39. Agnes Herbert, *Casuals in the Caucasus*, pp. 148–149.

40. Agnes Herbert, *Casuals in the Caucasus*, p. 155.

41. Agnes Herbert, *Casuals in the Caucasus*, p. 266.

42. Agnes Herbert, *Casuals in the Caucasus*, p. 185.

43. Agnes Herbert, *Casuals in the Caucasus*, p. 314.

44. Book review in *Booklist*, Vol. 8, Dec. 1911, p. 148.

45. John C. Phillips, *A Bibliography of American Sporting Books* (New York: James Cummins Booksellers, 1991), p. 170.

46. The plates noted are in Herbert's, *Two Dianas in Alaska*, facing pages 120 and 290 and corresponding to plates facing pages 139 and 218 in Captain C. R. E. Radclyffe's, *Big-Game Shooting in Alaska* (London: Rowland Ward, 1904).

47. The portrait of the Leader faces page 241 in Herbert's, *Two Dianas in Alaska*.

48. Phillips, *A Bibliography of American Sporting Books*, p. 170.

49. Phillips, *A Bibliography of American Sporting Books*, p. 353.

50. Maria Aitken, *A Girdle Around the Earth* (London: Constable, 1987), p. 10.

51. Maria Aitken, *A Girdle around the Earth*, p. 95.

52. See, for example, *Who Was Who. A Cumulated Index, 1897–1980* (New York: St. Martin's Press, 1981).

Nora Gardner accompanied her husband to India on a sporting expedition in the early 1890s.

Accompanied by a few friends, Isabel Savory traveled to India where she hunted wild goats, bears and tigers.

In a fanciful illustration from her book, A Sportswoman in India, Isabel Savory aims at tigers while precariously perched in a tree stand called a machan.

Agnes Herbert represented the adventurous spirit of women big game hunters, writing of her exploits in Africa, Alaska and the Caucasus.

Unprepared for the dangers of African travel and hunting, Marguerite Roby sparred with illness and rebellious porters in addition to wild game.

Delia Akeley saved her husband Carl Akeley's life when he was mauled by an elephant, but after their divorce, she received little recognition for her exploit.

Grace Gallatin Seton was introduced to hunting by her husband Ernest Thompson Seton. She later went on her own hunting trips to India and South America.

Novelist Mary Hastings Bradley wrote three books of hunting experiences in Africa and Asia. Moments after this photo was snapped, the "dead" lion suddenly came to life.

Aboard the "Northern Light," Courtney Borden and her husband enjoyed hunting big game including polar bear in Arctic seas.

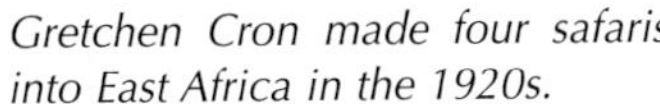

Gretchen Cron made four safaris into East Africa in the 1920s.

Minnesotan Grace King poses next to a wildebeest she bagged in Kenya.

Combining personal charm and courage, Osa Johnson was as at home with a rifle in her hands as she was with a camera or baby antelope.

Gladys Harriman represented an era of affluent hunters flying to their hunting venues. Here she poses with a trophy bighorn ram.

A photo appearing in Two Dianas in Alaska, *of a moose supposedly shot by Agnes Herbert. Compare it to the photo of C.R.E. Radclyffe and his moose published five years earlier in Big Game Shooting in Alaska.*

The original photo showed a calm Captain Radclyffe posed next to the moose he had bagged.

SIX

Dianas on Peaks, Prairies, and Polar Seas

> The clearest and simplest manner of describing a journey of exploration, of sport, or of adventure, is often in the form of the original diary—penned *in situ* from day to day in the tent, the forest, or the canoe, on the shore, the glacier, or the mountain side.[1]
>
> H. W. Seton Karr, 1887

Big game hunting trips to the Rocky Mountains, British Canada, and the Alaskan wilderness gained great popularity in the late nineteenth and early twentieth centuries. The remote regions of the North American continent provided locales far distant from the bustling centers of civilization. The northern frontiers, accessible by exhausting travel by boat or canoe, coupled with strenuous portaging, pitted the hunter's strength and fortitude against lands locked in snow and ice for large parts of the year.

The landscape also revealed a rich variety of big game animals. Species of wild sheep and goats abounded in the Rockies and ranges farther north, while varieties of grizzly, brown, and polar bears extended from the mountains of the United States to the polar regions of Alaska and Canada. Moose, elk, and caribou seemed to exist in numbers rivaling the antelope of Africa or Asia. Books penned by famous sportsmen such as Frederick Selous, Captain Radclyffe, Colonel Claude Cane, and Charles Sheldon ably described the region, its human inhabitants, the climate, and the excitement of the hunt.[2]

Women hunters also journeyed to the high latitudes of the Western Hemisphere and to the polar regions north of Europe. They faced, in general, a greater adaptation to a land of weather extremes when compared to India or Africa. The subarctic environment in autumn and early winter, prime hunting seasons, could prove as dangerous a foe as a wounded bear. When Agnes Herbert traveled to Alaska to collect big game trophies, she soon discovered a need to adapt to the harsh climate of the northland. When her hunting party purchased fur costumes similar to those worn by Eskimos and Aleuts, she deemed the most useful garment to be the parka which consisted of "a whole skin coat with a hood to it and no opening down the front, the coats being pulled over the head like a jersey."[3] Parkas were usually made of caribou or marmot skins with the fur worn on the outside. She also marveled at the decoration worked into the hides by native women using animal sinews in place of thread, and ivory needles.

MRS. SUSAN ST. MAUR

In the period from 1880 to 1940, a mere handful of women recorded their big game hunting expeditions in North America and subarctic Europe, and these trips were almost always in the company of spouses or other men. Perhaps the earliest account of a sporting trip to this region by a woman was titled *Impressions of a Tenderfoot, During a Journey in Search of Sport in the Far West* (1890), by Mrs. Algernon St. Maur. Born Susan MacKinnon in the 1850s, she married Algernon St. Maur, the fifteenth Duke of Somerset, in 1877. The Duchess and her husband departed from Liverpool in May 1888, "in search of health, sport, and pleasure" in British Columbia.[4] Algernon St. Maur had been stationed in Canada during the Riel Rebellion of 1870 and wanted to return to fish and hunt big game. After crossing the Atlantic, the couple traveled up the St. Lawrence River to Quebec, then proceeded by rail to Winnipeg and Calgary. The flatlands leading to the rise of the Rocky Mountains stretching into the distance left the woman nearly speechless. "I felt all the exhilaration that freedom gives in these untrodden solitudes," she penned in her notebook.[5]

At Banff, the St. Maurs enjoyed horseback riding into the timber country and fishing in local lakes. A monster trout weighing twenty-eight pounds was taken, as were many smaller ones. The large trout was carried to the hotel in Banff for special preparation, while other meals were prepared over an open fire on the lakeshores. Later, while traveling and fishing through the mountains, Susan St. Maur was introduced to the sport of trolling for trout with a spoon. "Trolling is not the same pleasure as fly-fishing," she noted. "There is no skill required in drawing in hand over hand on a strong line a three or six pound trout; but we, being hungry, were glad to get them."[6]

St. Maur and her husband traveled up Canadian rivers in search of better fishing grounds. When impassable rapids were encountered, portaging canoes and supplies over fallen logs and slippery riverine rocks was required. She noted the agility of the Indian guides as they maneuvered the canoes to safe landing spots, then manhandled the craft and bundles around the rapids. Having to fend for herself, she followed suit. "I was glad my tweed petticoat reached only to my knees," she later penned, "and with long boots, a flannel shirt, and Norfolk jacket, I could jump from rock to rock in a way that surprised even myself."[7] The woman's hunting clothing made an impact on a local miner who expected her to be dressed in brightly colored silk gowns befitting a member of the English nobility. "We took the greatest trouble to procure sufficiently rough clothes for the life out here," she admitted, "and wear the same day after day."[8]

St. Maur soon discovered that North America, while lacking the deadly mosquitoes and other insects of the tropics, maintained its own legions of pests. While camping in the British Columbian forests, she regretted leaving cumbersome, boxy mosquito masks behind in Vancouver as clouds of the buzzing insects descended on her campsite. Lying in the still air of the tents was an impossibility. She resorted to sleeping on nearby rocks, where a gentle breeze provided some relief. Even pulling silk bed clothing over her head did not provide adequate protection. By morning, her face "was very much swollen from mosquito bites, but carbonate of soda with a little water, dabbed on gently with the aid of a bit of cotton wool, at once removed all irritation."[9]

By October, Algernon St. Maur had taken up the hunting trail in pursuit of moose and bear. His wife, intent on getting in a bit of hunting as well, armed herself with a small-caliber Colt revolving rifle. She stalked wolves but "did not get a shot, these animals being most wary."[10] Compounding her lack of sporting adventures were the discomforts of the frigid British Columbian nights. While staying in a cabin near Findlay Creek, she woke one morning to find the water in her basin frozen and her sponge the consistency of a rock. She relied on the small pleasure of a well-heated hot water bottle while her husband was away.

Collecting big game, however, turned out to be a disappointment for the couple. Despite numerous stalks in British Columbia, Alberta, and Manitoba, little of consequence was bagged. By December the St. Maurs were in New York for the voyage home. While she had enjoyed her Canadian adventure, the prospects of returning to England left her quite happy. "To thoroughly enjoy home one must travel," she entered into her notebook, "and when far away by comparison realized the rest, the comfort, and the repose which one finds in no other place."[11] Susan St. Maur continued to travel but found the comforts of life in England to be decidedly her preference. She died in 1936.

ELINOR PRUITT STEWART

Unlike Susan St. Maur, who was a casual visitor to North America, Elinor Pruitt Stewart followed her marriage and her pioneering spirit to live and work in the western United States.[12] Born in Arkansas in 1876, she spent most of her childhood in Indian Territory (Oklahoma). After her marriage and the untimely death of her husband, she traveled to Wyoming in 1909 and witnessed some of the bitter range wars wracking the region. During her travels in the West, she kept copious notes, penned letters, and wrote numerous articles for local newspapers. Her first book appeared in 1914 as *Letters of a Woman Homesteader*. While the bulk of her writings concerned her life and activities, she took time to include her memories of an elk hunting trip to the Rockies in *Letters on an Elk Hunt* (1915). Though her notes on hunting were relatively brief, her book captured the grandeur of the scenery and the powers of nature.

Following the lure of Wyoming's bull elk, Stewart's hunting party camped in a clearing surrounded by lofty pines. During the night, a huge thunderstorm whipped through the mountains—"flash after flash of the most blinding lightning, followed by deafening peals of thunder," she wrote. There was no rain or wind in this storm, however, and Stewart worried that "had the lightning struck one of the big pines there would not have been one of us left."[13] Fortunately for the hunters, lightning struck towering trees far removed from the group.

Even more awesome than the thunderstorm that had threatened the camp was a landslide. When elk were sighted the day after the storm, the booming reports of several of the hunters' rifles caused two huge stones to tumble down. Stewart watched in disbelief as a nearby grove of aspen began moving faster and faster, with an accompanying collection of stones and dirt sliding into the river below. The rifle blasts had caused the landslide.

While Stewart was relatively familiar with firearms from her life in Oklahoma and Wyoming, she was surprised by the recoil of the .30 Krag military rifle she carried. Using a rock as a rest, she fired the rifle the moment a male hunting companion shouted at her to take a shot at an approaching bull elk. Obviously unfamiliar with the gun, she had not secured the butt tightly against her shoulder when she pulled the trigger: "Next I found myself picking myself up and wondering who had struck me and for what. I was so dizzy I could scarcely move," she noted in a letter. When Stewart returned to camp, she was stiff and sore. "Next morning," she recalled, "my jaw and neck were so swollen that I hated any one to see me, and my head ached for two days."[14] She had also missed her elk.

Stewart returned from her hunting trip and continued to write a series of articles and columns, though few reflected any further hunting activities. In 1926 she was run over by a haymower when a covey of prairie chickens suddenly flew up and spooked her horses. She never fully recovered from the accident. Elinor Pruitt Stewart died in 1933.

MABEL MORGAN BOVET

Californian Mabel Morgan Bovet joined her husband, Louis A. Bovet Jr., on a moose hunting trip in the Alaskan hinterland in 1931. The couple traveled from their home in San Mateo to San Francisco, then by steamship to Victoria. Transferring to another vessel bound up the Inland Passage to Seward, they eventually reached Anchorage via rail. They boated and packed to the Kenai Peninsula, reaching their moose hunting camp, where low, rolling hills, bogs, and aspen forests met. Even as camp was established, bull moose could be heard clashing in combat over females. As night descended, Mabel Bovet feared that nearby moose would trample their tent.

Mrs. Bovet had little experience in hunting big game, let alone moose in the Alaskan wilds. When the opportunity was presented to shoot at a large bull nearly four hundred yards away, she opted to hold her fire: "Never having qualified as an expert with the rifle, I naturally had my doubts."[15] On another occasion, she left her rifle propped against a tree as she crawled with her guide to inspect a trophy bull. When the target was sighted, the surprised guide asked her where her firearm was. Bovet explained that her husband had instructed her to imitate the guide in every respect. When the guide leaned his rifle against a tree, "I likewise had done so!" she explained. By the time the rifles were retrieved, the moose was out of sight.

Bovet steadfastly slogged through swamps and willow thickets in search of a true trophy animal. Smaller bulls were bypassed as she was determined to bag a larger specimen. After missing a huge bull, she finally bagged her trophy, then celebrated: "Indeed, I could hardly wait to see my husband to tell him the good news!"[16] She recalled her moose hunt in a brief chapter titled "My Initiation to Big-Game Hunting," which appeared in her husband's book *Moose Hunting in Alaska, Wyoming, and Yukon Territory* (1933).

MARJORIE WIGGIN PRESCOTT

Canoeing, portaging, and camping were also elements of Marjorie Wiggin Prescott's Canadian trip after moose. She accompanied her husband, Shelburne Prescott, and assorted friends to Nova Scotia and Newfoundland in the mid-1930s. At the Canadian settlement from which they would canoe into the interior, she recalled luxuriating in a hot, soapy bath for as long as she could, because "it had to keep me ten days." The hunting experience was new for her, though she realized that her husband's passion for sport was one she would have to share or be left behind. "I carried a rifle wherever I went and felt important into the bargain," she later wrote. When her hunting party was portaging from lake to lake, she began to realize the extent of the gear they carried. "Soon I was not useful enough in being merely the gun bearer, so fishing rods, cushions and sweaters were added to my load; I was everlastingly catching the rods in the bushes and then having to back out carefully and repoint myself along the trail." On the return trip, a day of strenuous portaging left Prescott and her partners drained. After several trees were felled for a campfire, there was sufficient energy to erect one tent—Prescott's. The woman gladly moved her sleeping bag to the edge of the tent, noting "that night five of us slept in a row, our feet stretched in the direction of the fire."[17] While the party enjoyed the outdoor activities, moose hunting turned out to be a failure.

Prescott penned three slender works detailing her experiences, all privately printed and limited to 150 copies. *Tales of a Sportsman's Wife* (1936) recounted the moose hunting expedition. Subsequent books included *Tales of a Sportsman's Wife: Fishing* (1937) and *Tales of a Sportsman's Wife: Shooting* (1939), capturing her travails with fishing rod and shotgun, respectively.

GLADYS F. HARRIMAN

Gladys F. Harriman, a friend of Marjorie Prescott's, also wrote a series of privately printed books detailing her sporting excursions. A New York socialite, Gladys Fries married E. Roland "Bunny" Harriman in 1917, a member of a wealthy and prestigious family that featured her new brother-in-law, noted diplomat and governor of New York W. Averell Harriman. Gladys seemed to prefer outdoor activities and relished the coming of the hunting season each autumn. She and her husband hunted deer in the hills near their home in Arden, New York, and were experts with the fly rod as well. The lure of the wild, however, beckoned the couple to game fields in the American west, Canada, and Europe.

In the early 1930s, Gladys and Bunny Harriman made the first of several trips to the Salmon River region of Idaho and into the Rockies of Wyoming. Determined to bag a mountain goat, Gladys Harriman failed for three successive years. On her fourth hunt, she finally spied an elusive goat on a distant ledge. Her male companions offered plenty of advice during her stalk of the prey before she finally told them to shut up. With her heart almost "choking" her "it galloped so fast," she fired.[18] Apparently her first shot hit the goat but failed to bring it down. She fired again, killing a nearby female goat. One of her guides tracked the wounded male as it climbed the rock chimneys, discovering numerous pools of blood as it fled. When night fell, the goat was still unsecured but promised delivery in the morning. To the horrified woman, however, sunrise unveiled a snowstorm that continued for three days. With snowdrifts waist deep, the goat was lost and so was Harriman's best chance to break her unlucky streak.

In 1934 the Harrimans traveled to Scotland to enjoy shooting driven grouse. Gladys Harriman, however, wanted to bag a red stag in the Highlands. Accompanied by McLeod, her stalker, she soon discovered the intricacies of maneuvering through difficult terrain and shifting wind conditions. To approach the herd of deer, she crawled through a sodden heather until her "neck ached so acutely that you finally gave up and let your face flop on the ground, which resulted in icy water oozing rapidly down your front."[19] With her teeth chattering and fingers numbed by the cold, she crept within one hundred yards of the stag, then was forced to wait as a heavy fog descended. Finally a breeze dispersed the fog, the stag leaped to its feet, and she fired. A tearful McLeod clapped her on the back and begged her permission to light his pipe in celebration.

During a subsequent trip to Austria, Harriman was paired with an elderly *jager* to hunt chamois in the Alps. Accustomed to carrying her own rifle during her Rocky Mountains trips, she was a bit flustered by Austrian sporting traditions. The *jager* carried the loaded rifle until game was sighted, then stuck his alpen stock in the ground to form a shooting rest. Only upon his direct command could the shooter fire. When a trophy chamois was sighted and the command to fire given, she pulled the trigger and watched as the chamois plunged into a narrow crevasse. She tried to prevent the *jager* from attempting to retrieve the animal from its dangerous perch, then watched in horror as the old man nimbly climbed. Within an hour, he had retrieved the chamois.

During another Alpine foray, Harriman and her new *jager* were about to hunt additional chamois when a large stag suddenly began to roar. The *jager* directed her to pursue the deer and maneuver into shooting range. As they waited for the stag to appear, an avalanche shattered the stillness:

> Suddenly something snapped and the whole side of the mountain at the head of the basin broke loose; snow poured down to the valley, great boulders rattled off leaping and bounding through space, the noise of their descent reverberating through the stillness like an angry animal. I sat spellbound and awe struck, overwhelmed by the grimness of nature. That particular spot was where we would have been had we carried out our chamois hunt.[20]

Though shaken by the experience, Harriman managed to bag her trophy stag.

In the fall of 1937, the Harrimans traveled to the Crystal Creek region of Wyoming to hunt bighorn sheep. Gladys was presented by her husband with a new 30.06 custom Springfield rifle. "From now on I knew that any misses were my fault," she noted in her diary. "The gun shot where you held it, and had plenty of shocking power to bring down any animal."[21] Fortunately for Harriman, her new rifle performed admirably as she collected a mature ram.

A year later, the Harrimans were aboard a seaplane headed for British Columbia for a twenty-one-day trip to hunt wild sheep, caribou, and mountain goats. Accompanied by their daughters, Betty and Phyllis, the hunting party packed by horseback along the Sikanni River. Gladys Harriman's diary reflected the changing landscape as their caravan wound its way through deep brush called shintangle and into timbered areas. Clouds of gnats and mosquitoes plagued the group until the coolness of autumn evenings finally drove the insects away. Dust and heat left the party feeling drained. Harriman felt the river offered the best chance for refreshment: "I jumped into the river and the icy water bucked me up no end," she jotted in her diary, though the guides "thought I was quite crazy."[22]

As they scrambled among the ridges and peaks of the region, they spotted game. On one occasion, Gladys Harriman used a scope mounted on her rifle to fire at a stone sheep, but her miss prodded her to remove the scope and opt for her more familiar open sights. Her choice ultimately paid off. While crouched on the slope of another mountain, she spied a ram and fired. Her trophy was one of several also collected by her husband and daughters.

The grandeur of the Rocky Mountains provided an allure to numerous hunters, including Gladys Harriman. As her hunting party prepared to depart, she soliloquized in her diary: "The mountains were more glorious than ever, full of lights and shadows they seemed to be beckoning us to come back to them. How I hated to see them fade and how dismal it made me realize that it would be another year at best before we could once more live again those heavenly days that end up around the camp fire. This kind of life is such a definite part of me now and nothing else can take its place."[23]

Harriman wrote three books recounting her sporting adventures, all of which she published privately in small numbers for friends and family. Her first, *A Journey of Adventure*, recalled her travels to Mexico, but with only brief comment on her hunting and fishing experiences. In *B.C. in A.D. 1938*, she described her shooting trip with husband and daughters to British Columbia after wild sheep and mountain goats. A third book, *"Mulligan,"* not only recapped the British Columbia expedition from 1938 but also revealed her earlier trips to Idaho, Wyoming, Scotland, and Austria. During and after World War II, she was active in the Red

Cross and other charitable organizations. She became an expert at riding trotting horses, a sport that seemed to fill her life in place of hunting with a rifle.

BETTIE FLEISCHMANN HOLMES

While sporting trips in the Rockies of Canada and the United States offered adventure and excellent sporting opportunities for women, perhaps the most daunting high-latitudes hunting trip was by steam yacht to the polar seas. Yachting cruises after Arctic big game in the frigid waters north of Scandinavia had been the hallmark of such famous English sportsmen as Captain Clark Kennedy and James Lamont in the nineteenth century, and the Duc d'Orleans in the early twentieth century.[24] Yachting operations were complicated affairs requiring the outfitting of the vessel, the hiring of a crew, and the preparation for the hunt itself. The guiding of the yacht among treacherous ice floes presented an additional yet necessary hazard, as seals and polar bears were known to haunt those venues.

Only a few women embarked on Arctic cruises after large game animals. In 1906 Bettie Fleischmann Holmes joined her physician husband and twelve-year-old son, along with her brother, yeast magnate Colonel Max C. Fleischmann, and his wife, on a sporting cruise to the hunting waters north of Spitsbergen. The party's vessel was the 176-ton Norwegian barkentine *Laura*. Launched in 1868, the same year that Charles Fleischmann, Bettie's father, immigrated from Austria to the United States with live yeast plants in his pocket, the *Laura* sported sails and a low-horsepower engine Betty dubbed "pony-power."[25] Throughout the voyage, she kept a log of their activities.

Traveling by rail from Cincinnati to New York, Holmes and her family then embarked by steamship for Germany, meeting Max Fleischmann in Norway to complete their sailing preparations. With a Norwegian crew, the *Laura* departed from Tromso in mid-June 1906 to hunt musk oxen, walrus, seals, and polar bears near Spitsbergen, the east coast of Greenland, and Jan Mayen Land. In their armory was a .450

double-barreled rifle, several large-caliber Winchester rifles, and several Savage .303 lever-action rifles, the last to be used by Bettie Holmes, her son Carl, and her sister-in-law Sarah Fleischmann. Max Fleischmann later admitted that he and Christian Holmes had been criticized for taking their wives on a dangerous shooting trip, but the women were determined to be active members on the voyage.[26]

Though the *Laura* would be sailing in Arctic seas in the summer, warm clothing was still a necessity. Bettie Holmes noted that suits of corduroy and loden, the heavy woolen material generally associated with the Tyrol, were to form part of their hunting outfits. A negligee of chamois skin was considered an ideal choice for cool nights aboard the yacht. High-laced, hobnailed hunting boots large enough to fit over two pairs of socks would allow plenty of traction and warmth when stalking game on rocky islands or on ice floes.[27]

The *Laura* had been at sea for only a few days when it ran into heavy seas and large stretches of pack ice. Proceeding carefully, the vessel shipped its rudder, and a new one had to be temporarily constructed from a spar while the actual rudder was towed through the water by a rope. Gliding among icebergs, the vessel reached Spitsbergen only to have the rudder rope tangle in its propeller. Additional time was needed to unsnarl the line before proceeding into a sheltered bay to complete necessary repairs.

While at Spitsbergen, the men of the party tramped into the hill country and secured a number of reindeer. Bettie Holmes also spent time shooting geese and eider ducks with her brother. All hands were pressed into the service of skinning and preserving the numerous specimens of waterfowl the hunting party harvested. Occasionally species of seals were bagged either from a small rowboat, or from the deck of the *Laura*. Bad weather continued to haunt the shooting party. Fog and thick ice abounded. Bettie Holmes noted one cold, foggy encounter in her log: "In the evening the ice assumed larger and larger proportions until we were in the midst of a dense pack. The ever shifting ice, washed into fantastic shapes by the constant lapping of the waves and sometimes tossed by the storms into high, jagged masses, with always the same wonderful coloring, possessed a ceaseless charm."[28] Banging through ice floes, the

Laura sprang several protective metal plates on her bow and took on a trickle of water at the rate of about one foot per hour. The crew pumped the water out, repaired the leaks, and then shifted weight from the bow to raise the damaged section as "far as possible above the water line."[29] In addition, ice formed thickly on the rigging of the vessel.

By August the shooting party was reduced to relying on their canned and preserved food stores. The venison taken at Spitsbergen had all been eaten, as had the waterfowl and the meat from a polar bear Max Fleischmann had shot. As for seal, "the crew [enjoyed] the meat of the young seal," noted Bettie Holmes, "but I am afraid that it is a dish we should not greatly relish."[30]

Polar bears were soon encountered and bagged. In attempting to get closer to the bears, however, the yacht steered between threatening ice floes. While one bruin was winched aboard the vessel, ice pushed the bow toward a pocket that could mean floes pinching the ship and possibly damaging the propeller. The crew clambered onto the ice and physically pushed the bow out of harm's way. "After repeatedly starting and stopping we were finally free without damage to the ship," Holmes observed, "but realizing more fully than ever how much our safety depended upon the never-ceasing vigilance, judgment and experience of our officers and crew."[31]

As the *Laura* slowly maneuvered through the drift ice, more hunting opportunities were presented as seals were clustered on ice floes, and polar bears following the trails of the seals. Bettie Holmes shot several seals by lying flat on the forecastle with her rifle pointed over the gunwale, then raising her head and shoulders slightly to take aim. "The shooting of seal from the ship is fraught with . . . much excitement" she declared in her log.[32] Later, when she and Sarah Fleischmann bagged a pair of polar bears, she ebulliently noted that she was "elated and proud at having killed a polar bear, particularly because, so far as is known to me, no woman has before penetrated or hunted in these regions."[33]

Cruising past the Greenland coast and unable to penetrate the drift ice, the *Laura* continued its passage to remote Jan Mayen Land. The hunters bagged a few foxes and assorted birds, lost their hunting dog, and examined the abandoned buildings of an Austrian Arctic expedition that had camped on the island more than twenty years earlier. After eleven weeks at more than 75 degrees north latitude, the yacht was steered for Norway. Nearly two dozen polar bears had been bagged, as well as numerous seals, reindeer, and hundreds of birds and waterfowl. When the Holmes and Fleischmanns returned to the United States, Bettie Holmes had her logbook published in a limited edition to be given to friends and family.

LOUISE BOYD

Nearly two decades passed before a second woman ventured by yacht into northern seas after big game. In 1926, San Francisco socialite Louise Boyd traveled to Franz Josef Land in the Arctic Circle on the *Hobby*, a sealer made famous by Norwegian explorer Roald Amundsen.[34] Born in 1887, Boyd inherited her father's investment company, then chose to use her resources to explore the Arctic. The shooting trip in 1926 aboard the chartered *Hobby* was to collect polar bears. During her journey, she snapped numerous photographs of the landscape and fauna, a visual record used by the United States during World War II. By the time she returned to San Francisco, as many as twenty-nine polar bears had been bagged, with some accounts indicating that Boyd had done nearly all the shooting. In a 1963 interview, however, she noted, "People are always exaggerating . . . for instance, it's not true I shot 19 polar bears in one day. That's a crazy story. I think it was only five or six and that was for food."[35]

Boyd made a number of subsequent scientific trips to the Arctic, including an attempt to find the missing Roald Amundsen, whose plane went down in 1928. She explored the glacial coasts of Greenland and was rewarded for her efforts by having several topographic locations named after her. Boyd also received numerous decorations and awards from the Norwegian and Danish governments and became the first woman to be elected to the Council of Fellows of the American Geographical Society. The books and articles she published were of her explorations and observations of the Arctic rather than of her hunting trip. She died in 1972.

COURTNEY LOUISE BORDEN

A year after Louise Boyd's Arctic safari, Courtney Louise (Letts) Borden joined her husband as part of the Borden Field-Museum 1927 Alaska Arctic Expedition to collect fauna along the coast of Alaska. John Borden, a trustee of the Field Museum of Natural History in Chicago and Borden Condensed Milk magnate, had made previous sporting trips to Alaska in 1913 aboard the auxiliary schooner *Adventuress*, and again in 1916.

Courtney Borden had been exposed to her husband's passion for hunting and fishing soon after they were married. She decided to try her hand at outdoor sport. "It was going to be entirely different from anything I had ever tried before," she later recalled. "It would be an experience, an insight into a man's world and why many husbands spend autumn week-ends away from home."[36] Traveling to Saskatchewan to hunt ducks at the lodge of noted sportsman-author William B. Mershon, Mrs. Borden quickly discovered that a duck hunter's day started at 4:15 A.M. More observer than shooter, she enjoyed her trip. A year later, and after practice rounds of clay-pigeon shooting, she was on the Illinois River for autumn mallards. She bagged her first duck, then ebulliently recalled her gun and shooting prowess:

> It was a twenty-gauge Remington pump, thirty-inch full choke barrel. Easy to handle, well balanced. John had given it to me a short time before. . . . I used only three shells [in the gun] and this did not seem all out of proportion for a gunner who would probably take a week to get one day's limit. Besides, for a woman experiencing her first season of duck shooting my gun was inexpensive, and pleasant to use because of its lightness.[37]

Borden also fished for trout, grayling, and salmon in the western United States, Canada, and Alaska and participated in Saskatchewan grouse hunting.

Borden's greatest adventure, however, would occur on the voyage to Alaska. The thought of cruising for months through polar waters both fascinated and horrified her. Her husband suggested they hunt polar bears and walrus, with a side trip to Wrangell Island. " 'Only half a dozen ships have ever been there,' " he informed her. "You'd be the first white woman . . . do you still think you can make it?" The woman quickly agreed "or the summer would be spent alone, taking care of home and children," she later recalled.[38]

Unable to find a suitable ship in a short period of time, John Borden ordered a specially constructed 140 foot, two-masted schooner christened *Northern Light* to be built in California. The couple left their three children (including an infant) in Chicago in early April 1927, packing rifles and assembling polar gear. Besides the crew, they were accompanied by two married couples—friends from Chicago—Courtney Borden's friend Frances Ames, and a band of Sea Scouts, an organization similar to the Boy Scouts of America, but with special maritime training.

By the end of May, the *Northern Light* had coasted along the shores of British Columbia, then to Juneau and west to the Aleutian Islands. After bouts with seasickness, the hunting party decided to stalk game on one of the islands. Though it was early summer, the temperatures were still rather frigid. Courtney Borden described proper hunting costumes:

> We arrived in camp wearing our heavy Hudson Bay cloth trousers and rubber boots. An extra forestry cloth shirt, forestry cloth trousers, sweat shirt, pair of high boots, three pairs extra heavy socks, three pairs medium weight socks, and three pair woolen socks was each person's outfit. Also two pairs of woolen gloves, three sets of heavy woolen underwear, a cotton muffler to wear under the rubber coat, two small towels, one bath towel, and a wash cloth. Oilskins became our most valuable article of clothing as they were worn everyday for four weeks. Besides the small necessaries, we had extra sweaters and heavy coats for wear around the camp.[39]

Once in camp, the hunting party was at the mercy of the elements. Cold rain lashed the site and soaked everyone. Tents warmed by candlelight cut some of the dampness. Personal hygiene became problematic as well. After boots were oiled and guns greased from the day's hunt, showering was accomplished by means of standing in a laundry tub with a tin can of heated water as a shower head. "Bath salts, and a jade bath-tub could never have been as welcome as that bath in camp after miles of hard walking," Mrs. Borden admitted.[40] Morning ablutions were carried out at a nearby stream.

The damp conditions on the Alaskan Peninsula caused the hunting party's .30-caliber Springfield rifle stocks to swell and the sights to go out of adjustment. Courtney Borden also noted that the Lyman receiver sights of her rifle would rub against her trouser leg as she walked, twisting the sensitive windage and elevation knobs out of alignment. Each day, the rifles had to be re-sighted before heading on the hunting trail.

The hunting party's Aleut guides doubted not only Courtney Borden's hunting ability but also that of the other three women in camp. She was certain the guides "thought the four women were along for decoration never dreaming we meant business."[41] Target shooting quickly proved Borden could hold her own, but she still had to prove her physical prowess to her native guides. While pursuing brown bears, she and her Aleut guide Mike pushed through groves of alders, crawled down ravines, and leaped over streams. She continuously stumbled over hummocks and downed branches. "I was puffing so hard I could scarcely see twenty yards ahead," she noted in her journal. "My legs ached in every muscle from climbing . . . I tripped and fell. Each time this happened, and it occurred rather terribly often, the rifle fell also. Mike never knew how difficult it was for me. He was too intent, thank goodness, on finding the game."[42]

Borden's ultimate test came in trying to bag a massive brown bear. Her first shot missed, but her second wounded the big bruin. Before she could ram another cartridge into the chamber, the bear disappeared into the brush. Nearly in tears, she followed Mike as he attempted, unsuccessfully, to find the animal's trail. Heartbroken, Borden assumed it had made its escape. Though the sun was setting, the pair continued in the direction the bear had run. Suddenly the guide pointed to an alder thicket and hissed a warning at the woman: "Don't get scared. Take your time—and shoot!" Borden could see the huge brown mass in the dense thicket: "Some inner something caused me to raise the rifle, steadily, and aim at the same moment as the crippled bear—looking absolutely enormous—

emerged from the alders. The shot found its mark. I have never known why because I was far too frightened to know anything. The bullet had penetrated the vital organs behind the left foreleg."[43] She later likened the shot to accidentally sinking a long putt on the eighteenth hole in golf.

After bagging several bears, the hunters on *Northern Light* continued along the Alaskan coast, then sailed through the Bering Strait. Walrus were collected, but Mrs. Borden began to complain of the cold. "Often I crawled fully dressed into blanket sheets pulling five blankets over me," she noted.[44] After stops on the Siberian coast and the Alaskan village of Tikeraq, the hunters attempted to find an opening in the drift ice near Wrangell Island. More walrus were spotted, and Borden, clad in a white parka, paddled by kayak to get near enough for an accurate shot. Later, on Wrangell Island, Frances Ames and another of the women bagged polar bears.

The trip to the polar regions had been a success. Seven walrus and seven polar bears had been taken, their hides to be used in museum displays. Numerous bird species were collected as well. Courtney Borden, upon her return to Chicago, wrote *The Cruise of the Northern Light* (1928), based on the journal she kept aboard the yacht. Her husband privately issued his own record of the voyage as *Log of the Auxiliary Schooner Yacht Northern Light* (1929), in which he recounted some of his wife's activities as well.

Critical reviews of Courtney Borden's book were mixed. Arthur Warren, literary critic for the Nation, disparaged her adventure: "There is no hard life of the sailor in Mrs. Borden's narrative. It is the sea in silk pajamas."[45] But Fanny Butcher in the *Chicago Daily Tribune* was more congratulatory: "Mrs. Borden has made no attempt to embroider the simple narrative of the trip, nor to enlarge on the uniqueness of her position as the first woman ever to write of her adventure in the arctic."[46] Obviously Butcher was unfamiliar with Bettie Holmes's privately printed narrative.

When economic depression gripped the United States in the early 1930s, Courtney Borden and her husband looked for solace in the countryside. They purchased Glenwild, a plantation in southern Mississippi, that became a retreat from the grind of business life in the

North. The couple built a kennel and raised hunting dogs while enjoying sport after bobwhite quail on their estate. In 1933 she published her second book, *Adventures in a Man's World.* Subtitled "The Initiation of a Sportsman's Wife," the book revealed her growing love of the outdoors, reflecting on her early hunts and angling trips, the cruise of the *Northern Light*, and her new life at Glenwild. She seemed not to miss Chicago's fast pace and sophistication in the least: "Dogs, and guns, and hunting togs had already replaced fur coats and were becoming more important than a closet of dressed-up clothes. 'Mother has gone hunting,' my children now smile and say to any casual visitor who might be calling, and to them it seems little different than as though they had said, 'Mother is planting tulips.' "[47]

Borden received favorable reviews of her book in a number of newspapers and periodicals. The literary critic for the *Boston Transcript* described the book as "an interesting story of adventure in search of big game" and noted that "Mrs. Borden has told it with the cheeky camaraderie of the true sportsman."[48] In the *Book*, critic Paul Allen noted that Borden was too modest in her title and "that a woman who can shoot straight, grin when she misses, go head over heels down the rapids and bewail only the lost steelhead has proved that sport is by no means only a man's world."[49]

The seemingly carefree days of plantation life soon ended for the Bordens. *Adventures in a Man's World*, published in February 1933, did not reveal their crumbling marriage. On July 1 of that year, the couple was divorced. Less than a month later, Courtney Borden married the Argentine ambassador.

BESS KENNEDY

In contrast to the polar regions, the arid hill country of southern Texas presented hunting opportunities for Bess Kennedy. Married at age sixteen, and before she graduated from high school in the 1930s, Kennedy and her husband lived in a tent in the Texan chaparral. Both were employed by the U.S. Biological Survey to trap and hunt mountain lions, bobcats, and coyotes that preyed on local herds of cattle and sheep. A novice at camping and hunting when she married, Kennedy soon became an expert.

The paucity of water meant the young family had to conserve the precious liquid. Water was carried from a creek to their camp in five-gallon cans weighing more than forty pounds. Wasting water was wasting labor. "We heated water at an open fire for each bath and learned to bathe in a gallon of the precious stuff in our small tin tub," Kennedy recalled. "Our technique was to set aside a small jug of clear, warm water with which to rinse off the soap. We did not splash water in our camp. We treasured every drop."[50] The incessant wind and dust coupled with the physical labor of tramping through the wilderness and setting traps precluded any attempt at fashion. "No wave was left in my hair," Kennedy later noted, "and the polish had chipped off my nails when I worked with the shovel."[51]

While the semi-arid climate presented discomforts, occasional thunderstorms posed life threatening dangers. During one severe thunderstorm that battered their campsite, Bess Kennedy feared for her family. Branches thudded against their tent and wind gusts pitched rain through every crevice. "Then a maniacal blast slit our home from back to front, and the tent was almost on our heads," Kennedy recalled.[52] Fleeing the collapsing structure, Kennedy, clutching her daughter tightly, struggled against tornadic winds as lightning scourged the landscape. Eventually the Kennedys made it to the shelter of a rancher's bunkhouse.

Bess Kennedy, who had never shot a gun in her life until after she married, practiced incessantly with a .22 rimfire rifle. "Every tin can became a treasure," she wrote. "Every day I spent hours at target practice and liked it. I liked being accurate. Inside of two weeks my targets were riddled with enough holes to prove that I was getting in a fair number of shots."[53] She eventually graduated to a .30-30 Winchester lever-action rifle for mountain lion hunting.

Kennedy became adept at tracking and stalking mountain lions, bagging a number of the felines for the Biological Survey. During one episode, she chased a mountain lion into a heavy thicket of poison ivy, "the kind of spot I should gladly leave to rattlers and rats," she declared.

Kennedy's dog suddenly chased the lion, which sprang onto the low branches of a willow tree. She realized that her problem was to shoot the cat and miss the dog, which was leaping madly about the base of the tree. Taking careful aim with her .30-30 lever action, Kennedy fired: "Luckily, I had got in a death shot through the heart, which killed him instantly, else even in death throes he would have hurt my reckless dog."[54]

If mountain lions presented difficulties, so did other fauna indigenous to the region. While pursuing wolves Kennedy stepped on a rattlesnake. The reptile recoiled angrily, then began to move. Kennedy shot the snake, but the encounter left her cautious: "For the next week or more I looked before every step."[55]

Tenting in the Texas brush, however, underscored the delights of traveling to local towns and mingling with the people. Crossing the border, the Kennedys drove to a small Mexican town for an evening of dancing after weeks of mountain lion hunting. Bess Kennedy suddenly found the change in clothing styles from denims and boots to more fashionable wear a bit disconcerting. "The first feel of skirts rather than pants was queer, but it took me no time to get used to it," she later recalled.[56]

Kennedy recounted her adventures as a lion hunter in *The Lady and the Lions* (1942). Though the publication of the book was in the 1940s, the tale of a woman big game hunter was still treated as a novelty by critics. "*The Lady and the Lions* shows what a girl can do when she sets her mind—and her traps—to it. It is also a lively and unconventional bit of autobiography," wrote a reviewer for the *New York Herald Tribune Books*.[57] The *Library Journal* described the work as having "courage here in plenty and [in] a new field of literature."[58] Apparently the book was Bess Kennedy's only published work.

The rugged vastness of the Rockies, Texas, Alaska, and the polar regions, coupled with their varied fauna gave inspiration to numerous books of exploration and sport by a number of men spanning the late nineteenth and early twentieth centuries. As in previous eras and venues, however, women joined their husbands on their hunting expeditions yet, curiously, did not contribute their adventures in books save for the few presented in this chapter.

Mrs. Charles Sheldon, for instance, sailed with her husband for the coast of Alaska in 1909 to hunt bear and deer. Though she had little experience with rifles, she gamely trekked through the bogs and forests of Admiralty Island, wading through tidal currents and falling into icy streams. She bagged deer and fired at a number of bears. Her efforts were recorded by her husband in three chapters of his book *The Wilderness of the North Pacific Coast Islands* (1912), but those chapters do not, of course, reveal her emotions or thoughts.[59]

Likewise, Sally Clark accompanied her husband, noted taxidermist-sculptor-sportsman James L. Clark, on shooting and museum-collection expeditions to Africa, Alaska, and Canada in the 1920s and 1930s. She bagged moose, bears, elk, lions, and other game, all noted in James Clark's book *Good Hunting* (1966), but apparently did not record her personal adventures.[60]

Accessibility to the remote hunting grounds of Alaska and Canada remained virtually unchanged from the Victorian era to the middle twentieth-century. The railroad travel favored by Susan St. Maur was slowly replaced by air trips enjoyed by the likes of Gladys Harriman. But to get into the interior of the country still required backpacking, portaging, or traveling by horseback. Unlike Africa and India, where motorcars and trucks were changing the face and pace of big game hunting, especially after Word War I, the rugged vastness and solitude of the northern latitudes preserved a wilderness kingdom demanding hunters to be equally as rugged.

NOTES

1. H. W. Seton Karr, *Shores and Alps of Alaska* (London: Sampson Low, Marston, Searle & Rivington, 1887), p. vi.

2. For examples, see F. C. Selous, *Recent Hunting Trips in British North America* (London: Witherby, 1907); Capt. R. C. E. Radclyffe, *Big Game Shooting in Alaska* (London: Rowland Ward, 1904); Colonel Claude Cane, *Summer and Fall in Western Alaska* (London: Horace Cox, 1903); Charles Sheldon, *The Wilderness of the Upper Yukon* (New York: Charles Scribners, 1911).

3. Agnes Herbert and A Shikari, *Two Dianas in Alaska* (London: John Lane, 1909), p. 46.

4. Mrs. Algernon St. Maur, *Impressions of a Tenderfoot* (London: John Murray, 1890), p. viii.

5. Mrs. St. Maur, *Impressions of a Tenderfoot*, p. 48.

6. Mrs. St. Maur, *Impressions of a Tenderfoot*, p. 88.

7. Mrs. St. Maur, *Impressions of a Tenderfoot*, p. 94.

8. Mrs. St. Maur, *Impressions of a Tenderfoot*, p. 182.

9. Mrs. St. Maur, *Impressions of a Tenderfoot*, p. 145.

10. Mrs. St. Maur, *Impressions of a Tenderfoot*, p. 190.

11. Mrs. St. Maur, *Impressions of a Tenderfoot*, p. 279.

12. See Elizabeth Fuller Ferris's preface in Elinor Pruitt Stewart, *Letters on an Elk Hunt* (Omaha: University of Nebraska Press, 1979) for a more detailed appraisal of Stewart's life.

13. Elinor Pruitt Stewart, *Letters on an Elk Hunt* (Omaha: University of Nebraska Press, 1979), p. 96.

14. Stewart, *Letters on an Elk Hunt*, pp. 104–105.

15. Louis A. Bovet, *Moose Hunting in Alaska, Wyoming, and Yukon Territory* (Philadelphia: Dorrance & Co., 1933), p. 89.

16. Bovet, *Moose Hunting in Alaska, Wyoming, and Yukon Territory*, p. 92.

17. Marjorie Wiggin Prescott, *Tales of a Sportsman's Wife* (Boston: privately printed by the Merrymount Press, [1936]), pp. 11–14.

18. Gladys F. Harriman, *"Mulligan"* (no place, no date), p. 12. Morris Heller places the dates of publication of *"Mulligan"* circa 1940 and *B.C in A.D. 1938* circa 1939. See Morris Heller, *American Hunting and Fishing Books* (Mesilla, NM: Nimrod & Piscator Press, 1997), pp. 40–41. On the front endpaper of the copy of *"Mulligan"* used in this book is an inscription from Harriman to Marjorie Wiggin Prescott: "Mine aren't so good as yours, but they bring Merry Christmas and Happy New Year to you. Gladys. Christmas 1940." Harriman is referring to both Prescott's books and her own.

19. Harriman, *"Mulligan,"* p. 38.

20. Harriman, *"Mulligan,"* p. 45.

21. Harriman, *"Mulligan,"* p. 26.

22. Gladys F. Harriman, *B.C. in A.D. 1938* (no place, no date), p. 45.

23. Harriman, *B.C. in A.D. 1938*, p. 69.

24. For examples, see Captain Alex W. M. Clark Kennedy, *To the Arctic Regions and Back in Six Weeks* (London: Sampson Low, Marston, Searle, & Rivington, 1878); James Lamont, *Seasons with the Sea-Horses* (London: Hurst &

Blackett, 1861); the Duke of Orleans, *Hunters and Hunting in the Arctic* (London: David Nutt, 1911).

25. Bettie Fleischmann Holmes, *The Log of the "Laura" in Polar Seas* (Cambridge, MA: The University Press, 1907), p. 8.

26. Sessions S. Wheeler, *A Gentleman of the Outdoors* (Reno: University of Nevada Press, 1985), p. 16. For Max Fleischmann's recollections of the voyage, see Max C. Fleischmann, *After Big Game in Arctic and Tropic* (Cincinnati: The Jennings and Graham Press, 1909).

27. Holmes, *Log of the Laura*, pp. 5–6.

28. Holmes, *Log of the Laura*, p. 50.

29. Holmes, *Log of the Laura*, p. 57.

30. Holmes, *Log of the Laura*, p. 79.

31. Holmes, *Log of the Laura*, p. 90.

32. Holmes, *Log of the Laura*, p. 65.

33. Holmes, *Log of the Laura*, p. 93.

34. For a more detailed description of Louise Boyd's life, see Elizabeth Fagg Olds, *Women of the Four Winds* (Boston: Houghton Mifflin, 1985).

35. Quoted in Olds, *Women of the Four Winds*, pp. 238–239.

36. Courtney Borden, *Adventures in a Man's World* (New York: Macmillan, 1933), p. 3.

37. Borden, *Adventures in a Man's World*, p. 25.

38. Borden, *Adventures in a Man's World*, p. 90.

39. Mrs. John Borden, *The Cruise of the Northern Light* (New York: Macmillan, 1928), pp. 47–48.

40. Mrs. John Borden, *The Cruise of the Northern Light*, p. 52.

41. Mrs. John Borden, *The Cruise of the Northern Light*, p. 47.

42. Mrs. John Borden, *The Cruise of the Northern Light*, p. 75.

43. Borden, *Adventures*, p. 120.

44. Borden, *Cruise*, p. 176.

45. Book review in *Nation*, vol. 127 (Dec. 26, 1928), p. 128.

46. Book review in *Chicago Daily Tribune* (Nov. 24, 1928), p. 15.

47. Borden, Adventures, pp. 205–206.

48. Book review in *Boston Transcript* (March 25, 1933), p. 1.

49. Book review in *Book* (Feb. 19, 1933), p. 10.

50. Bess Kennedy, *The Lady and the Lions* (New York: Whittlesey House, 1942), p. 97.

51. Bess Kennedy, *The Lady and the Lions*, p. 105.

52. Bess Kennedy, *The Lady and the Lions*, p. 125.

53. Bess Kennedy, *The Lady and the Lions*, p. 39.
54. Bess Kennedy, *The Lady and the Lions*, p. 206.
55. Bess Kennedy, *The Lady and the Lions*, p. 176.
56. Bess Kennedy, *The Lady and the Lions*, p. 104.
57. Book review in *New York Herald Tribune Books* (Nov. 15, 1942), p. 49.
58. Book review in *Library Journal*, vol. 67 (October 1942), p. 844.
59. Charles Sheldon, *The Wilderness of the North Pacific Coast Islands* (New York: Charles Scribners, 1912).
60. James L. Clark, *Good Hunting* (Norman: University of Oklahoma Press, 1966).

SEVEN

Grace Gallatin Seton: A Diana in the Rockies

> "Plenty of women have handled guns and have gone to the Rocky Mountains on hunting trips—but they are not among my friends. However, my imagination was good, and the outfit I got together for my first trip appalled that good man, my husband, while the number of things I had to learn appalled me."[1]
>
> Grace Gallatin Seton, 1900

Like many women before her, Grace Gallatin Seton's interest in sporting activities grew largely due to her spouse's recreational preferences.[2] Born in 1872 in Sacramento, California, to Albert and Clemenzie Gallatin, she was the youngest of three children living in a prosperous household. When her parents divorced in 1881, she moved with her mother to New York City, later attending the Packer Collegiate Institute. In 1894, while on a cruise with her mother to Paris, she met Ernest Thompson Seton, soon to be considered one of America's premier naturalists and outdoors authors. The friendship blossomed, and they were wed two years later.

Grace Seton realized that if she wanted to play an active part in her husband's life, she would need to spend time hunting, fishing, and camping. Having had little experience with firearms or fishing rods, she gamely learned their use and joined her spouse on her first big game hunting trip to the Rocky Mountains in 1897. It was the first of many trips to both the American and the Canadian Rockies.

Riding sidesaddle was quickly ruled out by Seton as she traveled on horseback with her husband to the shooting grounds of the Rockies. Why wear "trailing skirts that catch on every log and bramble, and which demand the services of at least one hand to hold up?" she wondered.[3] Seton created her own divided skirts for riding astride a horse, complete with a five-inch stitched hem and with a length four inches above the ground. As for undergarments, she recommended wearing bloomers. Heavy-soled boots more than twelve inches high and a felt hat were also added to her costume. That image was important was reflected in her choice of jackets: "One that looks well on the horse is tight fitting, with postilion back, short on hips, sharp pointed in front, with single-breasted vest of reddish leather, fastened by brass buttons, leather collar and revers, and a narrow leather band on the close-fitting sleeves."[4] She also preferred a comely brown silk veil tied over her hair and tucked under her sombrero, which not only kept her hair out of her eyes, but also created a bit of a fashion statement: "Why look worse than your best at any time?" she mused.[5]

As the hunting party neared its destination, Seton admitted that her hair might turn white as she beheld the swift current of Idaho's Snake River. The hunters had already crossed several meandering bends of the river when she finally discovered the worst was yet to come. As their wagon of supplies crossed the "boiling, seething flood," the current swept the wagon sideways. With the team flailing madly for footing, Seton watched in horror as their rifles, fly rods, overshoes, and other items floated downstream. Fortunately, two men on horseback were able to direct the wagon team to dry ground and nearly all the supplies were rescued. "After that, earth had no terrors for me," she noted in her journal.[6]

Seton apparently had never seen big game bagged before. When her husband wounded a bull elk, he waited for it to clamber out of the lake before issuing a fatal shot. Grace Seton was beside herself with horror as the wounded animal struggled through the water, begging her husband to finish the job quickly. When he noticed her tears, he was sure she would be unable to shoot an animal. To his surprise, however, she asked where the best locations were to place a bullet so the animal wouldn't suffer. "My woman's soul revolted," she recalled, "and yet I was out West for all the experiences that the life could give me, and I knew, if the chance came just right, that one elk would be sacrificed to that end."[7] When she had her opportunity a few days later, she calmly and accurately dropped an elk at 135 yards, then admitted she felt little glory in her achievement.

Mountain fog hindered Seton's additional attempt to bag a bull elk, causing her to lose her way along treacherous mountain trails. The loss of direction, coupled with the realization of the immensity of the area, was almost overwhelming. The fog descended quickly, and "everything was swallowed up in a dark misty vapour that cut me off from every object . . . the ground at my feet [was] blurred," she recalled. Panic momentarily set in: "Regardless of possibly near-by elk, I raised a frightened yell. My voice swirled around me and dropped. I tried again, but the sound would not carry."[8] After she and her mount skidded down some loose gravel and came to rest against a boulder, Seton fortuitously bumped into her husband who had not heard her cries nor had an inkling that she had been lost. Her sense of relief was undoubtedly profound.

Being left in camp alone with only the cook as a companion, the woman was justifiably worried. The cook, "a grim silent mountaineer," had admitted to murder, robbery, barroom brawls, and poaching. The cook approached her tent, inviting her to sit by the fire since it was warmer than staying in the tent. With her husband and another shooting companion on the prowl in the mountains for game, she watched with uneasiness as the cook sharpened a fistful of knives, handling them "lovingly, [he] rubbed off some blood rust here and there, and occasionally whetted one to a still more razor edge and threw it into a nearby tree, where it stuck, quivering."[9] Her heart was in her mouth as the cook squeezed her arm, then motioned her to silence when he thought he heard a bear approaching. As the pair headed into the brush, Seton doubted the wisdom of her continuing. She sneaked back to camp where she armed herself with her .30-30, then commenced a bit of target practice to bolster her courage. When the cook returned to the camp, he tried his hand at target shooting with his revolver. The stunned woman, expecting the worst, was soon treated to the lonely cook blurting out the misfortunes and mistakes of his younger days. She was still listening to his tale of woe when the hunting party finally returned.

Seton also experienced her first mountain snowstorm. While on the track of a grizzly bear, she and her hunting party began a long ascent into the Shoshone Mountains between Idaho and Wyoming. As they neared ten thousand feet, heavy snow began falling. She felt as if she were freezing as snow whipped against her face and her feet went numb in the stirrups. When they reached their camping area, four feet of snow covered the ground. Even though her physical discomfort was extreme and she had to fight back tears, she realized the other members of the hunting party were hard at work shoveling snow, preparing a campfire, and tying up horses. She slumped near the fire, swallowing snow to assuage her thirst: "I felt stuffed with snow; snow water ran in my veins, snow covered the earth, the peaks around me. I was mad with snow. They gave me snow whiskey and put me beside a snow fire. . . . They put rugs and coats around me till I could not move with their weight; but they were putting them around a snow woman."[10] Her friends finally warmed her with soup and chocolate, the latter mixed with more whiskey.

If winter snows at high altitudes presented extreme physical discomfort, the Rockies in the summer also offered seasonal hazards. Half stupefied by Montana's torrid summer, Grace Seton suddenly stumbled on a rattlesnake coiled to strike. In a bemused fashion, she recalled that the best weapons to use against a snake were rocks or a forked stick while keeping a loaded revolver in reserve. Since she had neither rocks, stick, nor pistol, Seton desperately cast about for a means of defending herself. Partially hidden in the brush was a rusty iron frying pan thrown away by some earlier traveler. Darting to the pan, she grabbed its handle and smashed the utensil against the rattler. Over and over she wielded the iron pan, then fiendishly hefted the dead snake and removed its rattles.

Seton's adventures with transportation were also evident on a bear hunting trip in the Canadian Rockies. Riding in a wagon carrying supplies over one mountain, she noticed the narrowness of the treacherous trails. Suddenly, as the wagon ascended a steep incline, the horses began to balk. Despite the workings of the wagon brake by the driver, the vehicle began to slip backward. With a solid-rock wall threatening a rapid and uncontrolled descent, the driver tossed the reins to the woman as he strained against the brake. Seton, who had never driven a four-in-hand wagon (two pairs of horses), rapidly found herself in a dilemma:

> I grabbed the reins in both hands. There were yards of them, rods of them, miles of them—they belonged to a six or sixteen horse set. I do not know which. I sat on them. They writhed in my lap, wrapped around my feet, and around the gun against my knee, in a shapeless and dangerous muddle. Of course the reins were twisted. I did not know one from the other. I gave a desperate jerk which sent the leaders plunging to the right, where fortunately they brought up against the rock wall.[11]

Slowly the team began to pull the wagon up the trail with Seton plying the reins while the driver pressured the brake and cracked the whip. Through an agonizing and physically demanding effort, they managed to maneuver the wagon to the top of the mountain, where the hunting camp had been established.

Seton recorded three years of sporting trips in *A Woman Tenderfoot* (1900) with good humor and adventure. She was not afraid to show her inexperience in attempting to bridge her world as a socialite to the rough and tumble activities of her husband. "Though I am still a woman and may be tender," she wrote on the last page of her book, "I am a Woman Tenderfoot no longer."[12]

After the publication of the book, the Setons spent time at their home in Connecticut. A daughter, Ann, was born in 1904. But the hunting trail called the Setons again, and they departed on another series of trips into the Rockies and Canada.

Seton's second round of adventures featured far more travel and camping than hunting experiences. She described firing her rifle at a bear, missing the bruin, then preferring to watch it peacefully depart. While visiting the Crow Agency on the Rosebud in Montana, she smoked a pipe with famous chief Plenty Coups. In another episode, she tried reeling in a huge muskellunge, only to have the fish break the line as it neared her boat. While bathing in a mountain pool, she was surprised and horrified to see a bull snake at water's edge

But the beauty and raw power of the mountains continued to capture her imagination. During one excursion, her party came across a great forest fire that had been raging for days. To ride beyond the rim of the fire would have meant a long detour and delay. Choosing to trot through an area already burned but still smoldering, Seton was badly surprised when her horse suddenly jumped as a burning tree crashed to the earth. "The air was electric," she noted, admitting to hearing Richard Wagner's "Fire Music" in her ears as she struggled to control her steed: "We had gone over two miles, jumping, dodging, trotting and stumbling, throats and eyes smarting from the smoke until the two miles seemed twenty, when I saw that we were leaving the region of living fire and passing through a city of the dead."[13] Exiting the burning forest, Seton's group finally reentered the sweetness of the mountain air.

On one October moose hunt, the majestic picture of a massive bull moose framed by a panorama of forest and lake caused Grace Seton to pause as she aimed at the creature. Her guide told her to shoot quickly, but she purposefully fired low and into the water. Disdainfully, her guide brought her back to camp. Seton admitted she might have lost the admiration of the men in camp, "but the reward was great," she noted, " a picture for all time that never fails to thrill me with excitement of that wonderful moment when nature allowed me to take another lesson from her primer of the woods." A few days later she had another opportunity to bag a trophy moose, this time as it emerged from a bog. Standing in her canoe, she fired at eighty yards and watched the big creature drop. Wanting to make sure the moose was dead and not suffering, she slipped into the mud of the bog and battled her way close to administer the "finishing touch." "The icy grip of murderous intent relaxed and I felt once more human," she recalled.[14] The trophy moose head later adorned a wall in her Connecticut home.

Grace Seton's second book, *Nimrod's Wife* (1907), included her further adventures in the Rockies coupled with a chapter on photographing reindeer in Norway. The work was met with mixed reviews by the literary critics. The reviewer for the *Academy* took her to task: "This is a book to read; if you like books about hunting, without any adventures which give a distinct thrill."[15] A critic writing in the *Bookman* was less than enamored with her praise for her husband: "[This book] offers another study of feminine self-consciousness, superimposed, in this instance, upon a perverted, and, at times, amusingly naive hero worship."[16] The reviewer for the *Outlook* was kinder: "[Seton has] preserved the atmosphere of close companionship with woods and waters that, even to the uninitiated, what is after all the chief charm of sport with gun and rod is made quite clear."[17]

Seton worked very closely with her husband on a number of projects. Together they founded the Girl Pioneers, an organization of young women interested in camping and other outdoor activities, a group that would later be known as the Camp Fire Girls. She helped prepare his papers, and illustrate his books and provided support on his lecture tours. But she was interested in far more than simply being the wife of a noted author. When World War I erupted, she raised money for the French to purchase six transport trucks to deliver food and military supplies from Paris to the Western Front.[18] For her efforts, she received three decorations from the French government. Seton also worked for the British government, then sold Liberty Bonds in Washington, D.C.

Grace Seton's interest and activities also turned toward women's suffrage. She was active in the National Council of Women and the National League of American Pen Women. Her efforts for women's rights didn't remain contained in the United States. During subsequent travels, she journeyed to Egypt and China to gain firsthand knowledge of the status of women in those countries. Her non-sporting books, *Woman Tenderfoot in Egypt* (1923) and *Chinese Lanterns* (1924), recorded her travels and observations with emphasis on the needs for social reforms.

In 1925 Seton sailed for India and Ceylon (Sri Lanka). The trip was to combine vacationing with equal-rights campaigning and big game hunting. As she soon discovered, the venture would not be without danger. India was in the throes of demanding independence from Great Britain. While leaders such as Mohandas Gandhi advocated peaceful civil disobedience, the memories of bloody outbursts as had occurred at Amritsar in 1919 were all too fresh in many Indian's minds. Increases in communal violence flared, as did physical violence against British residents and other whites. Traveling by rail through the country, Seton was disturbed during the night by several native men trying to break into her compartment. Though she had been warned to firmly bolt her doors because of recent attacks by some Indians against Europeans, she had deferred, preferring the freedom to enter or leave her room at will. Momentarily bewildered, she managed to substitute wooden clothes hangers as a makeshift lock. "Thoroughly frightened I realized how murders are committed," she noted. "There was a very distinct desire for a revolver surging in my brain. In desperation, I grabbed a large electric torch and pulling up the blind of the carriage door to which the man was clinging, I flashed the light full in his face." Seton's would-be attackers abandoned their efforts and dropped off the moving train. Later in the night a group of four native men attempted to pry the lock but were summarily chased away by train guards.[19] When the train stopped at Ashmere, she decided to do a bit of sight-seeing, but when a hostile group of Indians nearly surrounded her, she beat a hasty retreat to the train station.

While in Ceylon, Seton opted for a chance to go elephant hunting. Though she was an experienced hunter in the United States, her nomenclature for a choice of firearms did not match that of a local outfitter. Though English was the tongue of exchange, the meaning of *gun* had different connotations: "In our free and easy America we do not hesitate to say gun for any kind of a weapon that kills, from a snub-nosed revolver to a Big Bertha," she glibly noted. "Not so with ye Englishman, Patron Saint of ye Sport. A gun is a cannon—big stuff, you know . . . and a gun can also be a shotgun. A rifle is never, never a gun, and even a shotgun that shoots shot out of one barrel and ball out of the same barrel is not a rifle. No indeed, it is a 'paradox.' "[20] In testing a .500 express double rifle for the first time prior to a tiger hunt, Seton was rocked by its recoil. "It had five hundred "kicks" thrown into one!" she reported. "I decided it would take a tiger in front to make me get behind it again!"[21]

She had to reacquaint herself not only with firearms but also with hunting clothing. Her lightweight garments of travel gave way to hunting togs that she was unaccustomed to wearing in the tropical Asian heat. "Instead of a few ounces of silk," she mused, "I was carrying pounds and pounds of khaki and wool, and felt and leather, and hardly an inch of it was dry." Her boots, as well, were "not a good fit, too large and incredibly heavy for feet accustomed to glove-fitting, paper-soled coverings."[22]

Though she was now properly garbed, British officials seemed less than enamored with the idea of an American woman hunting rogue elephant's in the Ceylonese jungles. "Why not be content with more ladylike sport?" growled one official.[23] Seton, however, was not to be deterred.

Other difficulties encumbered her hunt. Perched in a woven straw howdah atop an elephant, she tried to maintain a firm grip on both her gun and her camera. As the elephant passed through the forest, a nest of ants was disturbed. With ants swarming over her, Seton quickly ordered the mahout to stop the pachyderm so she could descend and rid herself of the stinging pests. Even as she tried brushing the ants off, shots from one of her party rang out in the jungle ahead. Quickly reclaiming her seat, she was panic stricken as her mount thundered forward at a dead run. Pitched from side to side, she left the dubious sanctuary of the howdah and clambered onto the elephant's head. Wrapping her legs around the startled mahout's waist, she clung for dear life: "No time for etiquette. That, or fall off!" Finally the elephant was brought under control and Seton's hunt continued.[24]

Seton's sporting adventures in India and Ceylon were hardly successful. Hunting tigers and elephants failed to produce the requisite trophy. She did note, however, that the equality of women even in big game hunting was sorely lacking. Hoping to travel to Nepal, she found the country closed to women hunters because a European woman had shot her beater instead of her quarry. A disgruntled Seton penned, "Her sex must suffer for the accident. A drastic order of exclusion was in force."[25] Upon her return to the United States, she published her experiences in *"Yes, Lady Saheb": A Woman's Adventurings with Mysterious India* (1925).

The book fared better among the critics than her earlier works, though the long-standing stereotype that women who achieved their goals were extraordinary remained. "How so much could have been crammed by one lady journalist into six months is a miracle even in this day of feminine prodigies," wrote the critic for the *New Republic*.[26] The reviewer for the *New York Times* waxed more artistic: "Mrs. Seton displays the colorful efficiency of an American painter, sympathetic, impressionist, rapid."[27]

With the Setons absorbed in their own interests and careers, the couple began to drift apart. In 1918, Ernest Seton met Julia Moss Buttree and hired her as his secretary. He sold his estate in Connecticut, preferring the open spaces of the southwest, where he built his retirement home near Santa Fe.

Continuing in her role as a globetrotter and activist, Grace Seton joined the Field Museum Expedition of 1926 to Brazil, Paraguay, Peru, and Bolivia. She studied Incan and pre-Columbian civilizations, and helped collect thousands of animal, bird, and fish specimens. Armed with a .30-30 lever-action rifle, she bagged Paraguayan crocodiles, wild pigs, and a variety of small game.

While Seton alludes to wanting to collect such South American creatures as tapirs and anteaters, her personal primary goal was to bag a jaguar, a wary beast, she described, "with forearms like steel traps, great muscles equal to a dozen prize fighters, poison claws and lightning speed."[28] Accompanied by several Paraguayan trackers with dogs, she rode into the thick jungles of the region, describing in detail the weather conditions and the terrain. When a jaguar was finally spotted and bagged, she refused to relate the details of "just how or when a bullet transformed this king of South American beasts from a magnificent jungle terror to a beautiful utilitarian trophy."[29] The details of her experiences, complete with her anticlimactic jaguar hunt, were published in 1932 as *Magic Waters: Through the Wilds of Mato Grosso and Beyond*.

Grace Seton returned from South America to continue her advocacy of women's rights. She actively supported Herbert Hoover's bid for the presidency in 1928, then served as the chairman of letters of the National Council of Women of the United States from 1933 to 1939. Her books remained popular, and she received a steady income from her lecture tours. By now, however, her marriage was in disarray. The enchantments of her hunting trips to the Rockies must have seemed a distant memory when she divorced Ernest Seton in 1933. A year later he married Julia Moss Buttree.

One more grand adventure awaited Grace Seton. She journeyed to Southeast Asia, but as a traveler, not a hunter. Her last travel book, *Poison Arrows: A Strange Journey with an Opium Dreamer through Annam,*

Cambodia, Siam, and the Lotus Isle of Bali, was published in 1938. Politics once more attracted her attention when she campaigned for Thomas Dewey in 1944. Her last book was a compendium of poetry and song for travelers.[30] Grace Seton died in 1959.

NOTES

1. Grace Gallatin Seton-Thompson, *A Woman Tenderfoot* (New York: Doubleday, Page, 1900), p. 16.

2. See also Marion Tinling, *Women into the Unknown* (Westport, CT: Greenwood, 1989). For a concise biography of Ernest Thompson Seton, see Lisa Knopp, "Ernest Thompson Seton," *American Nature Writers, Vol. II* (New York: Charles Scribners's Sons, 1996). Initially he was known as Ernest Seton-Thompson, then he changed his name (see Knopp).

3. Grace Seton-Thompson, *A Woman Tenderfoot*, p. 34.

4. Seton-Thompson, *A Woman Tenderfoot*, p. 27–28.

5. Seton-Thompson, *A Woman Tenderfoot*, p. 55.

6. Seton-Thompson, *A Woman Tenderfoot*, p. 69.

7. Seton-Thompson, *A Woman Tenderfoot*, p. 87.

8. Seton-Thompson, *A Woman Tenderfoot*, p. 136.

9. Seton-Thompson, *A Woman Tenderfoot*, p. 119–120.

10. Seton-Thompson, *A Woman Tenderfoot*, p. 202.

11. Seton-Thompson, *A Woman Tenderfoot*, p. 325.

12. Seton-Thompson, *A Woman Tenderfoot*, p. 361.

13. Grace Gallatin Seton, *Nimrod's Wife* (New York: Doubleday, Page, 1907), p. 120.

14. Seton, *Nimrod's Wife*, p. 381.

15. Book review in *Academy*, vol. 73 (Nov. 9, 1907), p. 107.

16. Book review in *Bookman*, vol. 25 (August 1907), p. 623.

17. Book review in *Outlook*, vol. 86 (June 29, 1907), p. 476.

18. For a record of Seton's activities in France, see Grace Seton, *Le Bien étre du blessé woman's motor unit New York women's city club: Report Dec. 1917 to Dec. 1919* (New York: no publisher, 1920).

19. Grace Seton, "*Yes, Lady Saheb": A Woman's Adventurings with Mysterious India* (New York: Harper, 1925) pp. 60–62.

20. Seton, "*Yes, Lady Saheb": A Woman's Adventurings with Mysterious India*, p. 133.

21. Seton, "*Yes, Lady Saheb": A Woman's Adventurings with Mysterious India*, p. 158.

22. Seton, "*Yes, Lady Saheb": A Woman's Adventurings with Mysterious India*, p. 136–137.

23. Seton, "*Yes, Lady Saheb": A Woman's Adventurings with Mysterious India*, p. 140.

24. Seton, "*Yes, Lady Saheb": A Woman's Adventurings with Mysterious India*, p. 161–2.

25. Seton, "*Yes, Lady Saheb": A Woman's Adventurings with Mysterious India*, p. 149.

26. Book review in *New Republic,* 45 (Dec. 16, 1925), p. 118.

27. Book review in *New York Times* (October 18, 1925).

28. Grace Seton, *Magic Waters* (New York: E. P. Dutton, 1933), p. 157.

29. Seton, *Magic Waters*, p. 178.

30. See Grace Seton, *The Singing Traveller* (Boston: Christopher Publishing House, 1947).

EIGHT

Of Champagne Safaris: Dianas in the Inter-War Years

> "Some one has said that hunting big game in Africa is a brutal sport and lacking in appeal to the woman of refinement . . . [but] as far as brutality is concerned, what is the difference whether you eat the flesh of a wary, watchful wild animal, killed by your own rifle or that of the pampered, unsuspicious, domestic animal slaughtered by some one else."[1]
>
> Grace King, 1926

The era of privilege and imperial power known by the likes of Florence Dixie, Nora Gardner, and Agnes Herbert was on the wane after the Great War ended in 1918. Though colonies would continue to be ruled by England, France, Belgium, and other European powers, the war had decimated treasuries, slaughtered millions of young men, engendered political revolutions, and provided the impetus for African and Asian independence movements.

Women's rights, too, had changed dramatically. Canada, Poland, and Germany granted women's suffrage in 1918; India, Austria and the Netherlands a year later. American women received the right to vote in 1920. It wouldn't be until 1928, however, that Great Britain would finally grant complete women's suffrage.

The experiences and literature of women big game hunters was changing as well. Whereas women had either traveled alone like Agnes Herbert, or accompanied spouses to military outposts, like Mrs. Baillie, the decades after the Great War featured safaris and shikar as ways of spending leisure time. Well-heeled Americans, enjoying economic success after the war, began making greater inroads into the traditional shooting grounds of Africa and Asia. Wife-and-husband teams embarked on fast cruise ships or airplanes to reach distant locales that had previously taken weeks or months of travel. Outfitters provided catalogs of necessary equipment ready to order from the comfort of home. As regional governments continued to develop game laws and licensing, former ivory hunters became professional guides.

Once the hunting parties arrived on their continent of choice, a caravan of trucks and cars ferried them into the interior. While old-fashioned safaris consisting of more than a hundred porters occasionally ventured to prime hunting venues on foot to collect trophies or museum specimens, most columns numbered about twenty camp workers, skinners, cooks, and gun bearers. Trucks carried tents, camp necessities, and luxury goods in addition to the working staff and the hunters. One author termed the era the period of "champagne safaris," where monied clients demanded that creature comforts accompany them into the field.[2]

Though travel and comfort had changed considerably, the experiences of women as big game hunters had not. The books they penned based on their journals and diaries reflected the same concerns and interests as had their sisters of the hunt in the nineteenth and early twentieth centuries. Descriptions of camp supplies, encounters with native tribes, and coping with tropical vermin and debilitating weather conditions remained in evidence. Cleanliness and clothing still were important components of their narratives. While modern rifles could kill more effectively than the black powder guns of the Victorian era, the experiences of women facing charging buffalo, elephants, or tigers still retained that spine-tingling thrill of danger and courage.

The numbers of big game hunting women increased dramatically as well. While actual statistics from the 1920s and 1930s are virtually impossible to obtain, the trend continued into the 1960s when one professional big game hunter noted that "over forty percent of big game hunting safaris include women clients."[3] Where books written by women in the Victorian and Edwardian eras rarely refer to a woman being injured or killed by big game (Agnes Herbert and Mrs. Baillie being the exceptions), the post-war decades reveal the human tragedy of hunting dangerous animals. In the 1920s, an Irishwoman named Mrs. Frank Green wounded a rhinoceros with her lightweight rifle, only to have the enraged animal later attack a car on a nearby rode and kill its driver.[4] Madame Deriddar, a Belgian woman, had wounded several lions, one of which turned on her, mauling her severely before she could pull out her revolver and kill the feline.[5] A woman named Mrs. M. Green of Kenya Colony was trampled to death by a rhinoceros she had wounded. Another hunter surmised that had Green "been more skilled in the use of a rifle this terrible tragedy might have been averted."[6] A few years later, Kathleen Bailey was badly mangled by a wounded rhinoceros she had shot.[7] Despite these dangers, women were traveling to hunt big game and writing of their adventures in greater numbers.

VIVIENNE DE WATTEVILLE

Personal tragedy and loss stalked Vivienne de Watteville on her first safari to Africa. She was still in high school when her father, Bernard de Watteville, embarked on a two-year journey through northeastern Rhodesia to collect specimens for the Berne Museum of Switzerland. In 1923, he was ready to return to Africa with his daughter, now in her twenties. By June the de Wattevilles were in Kenya. Their goal was to collect a variety of animals with an eye toward bagging an elephant for the museum, despite their lack of experience in skinning and preserving large hides. Their safari traveled on foot without benefit of motorized vehicles, which were already becoming popular.

The young woman's initial experience with shooting animals left her horrified. After her father had bagged an antelope, she wished his aim had been off. The longer they remained on the shooting grounds, however, the greater her metamorphosis. She admitted to relishing roasted liver from a fresh kill, and eating biscuits, and smoking hand-rolled cigarettes even though her arms and hands were covered in blood from the butchering and skinning process.

While Vivienne de Watteville became adept at skinning specimens, her father did the bulk of the hunting, securing elephants, buffalo and numerous lions, as well as other game. So plentiful were the felines that when a canvas bathtub disappeared from their camp, the woman blamed a porter for leaving it behind. The porter quickly displayed saliva-slathered canvas remnants and bits of chewed rope. A few days later, the hunting party discovered "lion droppings in which were three fair-sized nails and a piece of [canvas] sacking."[8]

It was a lion that changed Vivienne's life forever. Bernard de Watteville had been stalking lions and had wounded one when the great cat suddenly sprang at him. It savaged his arm and sank its claws into his legs before he could finally bring his rifle up under its jaw and kill it. Though Monsieur de Watteville had been badly mauled, he managed to walk two hours to return to camp. His daughter was aghast at his wounds: both legs with deep gashes and with muscles torn away—his arm ripped to the bone and his hand lacerated through. She cleansed her father's wounds, cutting away the damaged tissue. Though he rallied, Vivienne recalled, "at sundown his wide-open eyes were staring straight past me."[9] She buried her father, then admitted to a black wave of desolation sweeping over her. Stricken with spirillum fever, she and her party lost their way in the jungle.

De Watteville forced herself to hunt to supply her porters with meat, though she was not used to firing her father's heavy rifle. A slender woman, she struggled with the weight of the big .416 Rigby. As she approached a herd of buffalo, she noted that the "high grass compelled a standing shot and, the .416 being heavy for me, it took me some seconds to draw a steady bead."[10] When the buffalo she wounded galloped into heavier grass, she lost her nerve and wouldn't pursue it. Fortunately for her and the hungry porters, she managed to bag a trophy bull within a day. Her father had set out to collect museum specimens, and she was determined to complete his project.

Upon finally reaching civilization, de Watteville described her father's wounds to a local doctor but was only partially relieved when the physician explained her father could never have survived his injuries. Still ravaged by illness and self-doubt, she was finally snapped out of her funk by the beauty of the sun rising over a mist-shrouded hillside, small rainbows arcing in the moist air.

Vivienne de Watteville wrote of her experience in *Out in the Blue* (1927). She made subsequent trips to Africa, but no longer with a rifle. The camera and the pen became tools of her trade, as she explored the mountains of East Africa and observed the elephant herds. Her second book, *Speak to the Earth: Wanderings and Reflections among Elephants and Mountains* (1935), revealed her love of nature and wildlife. When *Out in the Blue* was reprinted in 1937, she noted in her preface that she believed "the public attitude towards big-game hunting has completely changed. The thrill of adventure cannot overcome the reader's distaste of killing."[11] Though she was tempted to rewrite the book and eliminate the hunting scenes, she determined that such a change would not have done her father justice. Vivienne de Watteville died in 1957.

MARY HASTINGS BRADLEY

While Vivienne de Watteville subsequently published two books of African adventures, Mary Hastings Bradley was already a well-known novelist when she embarked on the first of her big game safaris to Africa in the early 1920s. Born in Chicago and educated at Smith College, she also studied at Oxford. After marrying attorney Herbert Bradley in 1910, she began a long career of writing magazine articles and stories for such famous periodicals as *The Saturday Evening Post* and *Red Book* in addition to her novels.

Inspired by stories of African explorer Henry Stanley and the famous museum groupings constructed by taxidermist and sculptor Carl Akeley, she proposed a shooting safari to East Africa. Besides her husband, she brought along her five-year-old daughter Alice, and a nanny.[12] She was delighted at the simplicity of outfitting her safari by ordering from a catalog. "My lists ranged from hobnailed shoes and flannel shirts and khaki knickers to white crêpe and lace evening gowns," she noted.[13] Though her catalog order was lengthy, she still wondered how many hairpins she would need for the months to come in the Congo rain forest. As she quickly discovered, however, in the heat and humidity of the tropics fabrics rotted, boots carried extra skins of mildew and metal objects thickened with rust unless items were carefully monitored and cleaned. After a weeklong bout with fever near Lake Tanganyika, a period with daily afternoon thunderstorms, Mary Bradley finally felt strong enough to delve into her clothing bag. As she neared the bottom of the bag, she found the contents "green with mold—baskets and coin purses and a pair of my slippers."[14]

Bradley's safari, accompanied by the experienced Africa hand Carl Akeley, trekked into the rain forests of the Belgian Congo in search of gorillas and other game. Sometimes traveling by bicycle, other times on foot with Alice in a basket carried by a pair of porters, the caravan climbed the slopes of Karisimbi where gorillas were bagged. They encountered a huge column of safari ants that Mary Bradley described as "a racing mill stream of black waters."[15] Christmas Day for Alice consisted of a small party with gifts of modeling clay, an elephant hair bracelet made by Akeley, and picture books. After the celebration, the hunting party stalked buffalo for eight hours.

There is little doubt that recoil was of concern to some women hunters, though many did not mention it in their writings. Even with India-rubber pads placed on the buttstocks to help absorb recoil, the thrust of the rifle upon the shoulder when firing, particularly the larger calibers, was considerable. Mary Bradley noted the .475 double rifles employed by her husband and their professional hunters, but with her warning that "any gun of that type is considered too hard in recoil for a woman."[16] Her rifle of choice was a Springfield bolt-action repeater in 30.06 caliber, a firearm she even used against elephant, buffalo and lion though a .30 caliber was considered by many experts to be too small for dangerous game.[17]

Mary Bradley's encounter with a lion was particularly surprising. After she had apparently killed a male lion with her Springfield, she posed for a photograph with the head of the trophy in her lap. Suddenly the lion roared. A startled Bradley leaped away as Carl Akeley raced to the scene. Angrily he informed the shooting party that the lion might only be temporarily paralyzed. When a final shot was delivered, the lion leaped into the air before succumbing.

After returning to the United States, Mary Bradley recounted her experiences in *On the Gorilla Trail* (1922). The reviewer for the *Springfield Republican* reminded readers of the uniqueness of the woman big game hunter: "This is a first class volume of exploration with the added novelty of being presented through a woman's eyes and with the pen of an experienced writer."[18]

In 1924 Mary Bradley and her family returned to Africa. Though some friends were dismayed that she was taking daughter Alice again, she quickly calmed their fears with a simple reminder that "Alice was as safe in Africa as in Chicago. Safety means ceaseless vigilance in either case."[19]

Once more accumulating supplies and hiring porters to transport the goods, the Bradleys began their second safari. By the 1920s outfitters, through catalogs or retail outlets, were supplying hunting parties with virtually all their expedition's needs. Not only were selections of clothing, camp supplies and goods available in copious quantities but the outfitters also provided packaging in carefully weighed containers so as to conform to regulations about how much weight a porter should handle. "Everything was in tins," noted Mary Bradley as her safari left Nairobi, "in wooden 'chop' boxes, furnished with lock and key." Among her supplies were tins of Cheshire cheese, Keiller's marmalade, Heinz baked beans, and Primrose soap. Included with her tents were two toilet tents, four circular baths, and six enamel wash basins. In addition, there was a complete crate of medicinals including quinine, iodine, and "an endless supply of oxide adhesive tape."[20] As for the porters, the deeper the caravan trekked into the jungle, the greater the chance of desertion. Bradley noticed the number of men lining up for the evening meal was beginning to dwindle. "Midnight was the dangerous hour," she wrote. "Porters always sat up half the night around the fires in the huts, talking, talking, talking all about their troubles with the *wazungu*—the white men—and the work and the hardships ahead, and by midnight they would talk their courage up to the action point and dash out on the homeward way."[21]

Though she was by now an old hand at safari travel, tropical insect life presented new challenges to Bradley. Her encounter with legions of green flies resulted in a painful road accident. While she was guiding a bicycle along a path, the flies temporarily blinded her. Suddenly losing her balance as her feet slipped in a gash across the road, she crashed face first into the hardened mound of an anthill. While her ribs were bruised by the bicycle handlebars, her lower teeth were "lying like ten pins over each other." Pushing the teeth back into place, Bradley despondently mused that "anyone who can picture herself in Africa with two front teeth out and months and months from a dentist will know just how I felt at that moment."[22]

Despite her best intentions of maintaining a clean costume while hunting, there were times when Bradley simply grabbed what was on hand before heading for her shooting stand. On one occasion she realized that if game were bagged, a photo of her with a trophy might be snapped: "I pulled on the trousers of yesterday, still streaked with mud, a wrinkled shirt, and two puttees that didn't match. The fuzzy one didn't belong to me, anyhow. Dutifully I reminded myself that to-day I might shoot an elephant and be photographed with the luckless animal, but doggedly I went on with the havoc I was making of my costume."[23]

When it came to shooting big game, Mary Bradley displayed her own cool courage despite being undergunned with her .30-06 Springfield. On one occasion, she stood nearly in the shadow of an elephant when she fired, only to have the wounded beast disappear into the forest. Later, with a rhinoceros crashing through the brush toward her, she leveled her rifle and fired. Though she did not bag the animal, her great sense of relief was twofold: that she had survived and that she "hadn't run or dived into a rabbit hole or done anything else to disgrace my sex in trousers."[24]

Judging physical beauty and mannerisms based on a Western ideal was not uncommon among women travelers. Bradley's less-than-flattering descriptions of Congo tribesmen, coupled with discussions on Congo cannibalism, were in evidence after one shooting incident. After dispatching an elephant, Bradley was nearly overwhelmed by the spectacle of dozens of native men, women, and children swarming over, around, and inside the elephant's carcass: "Never have I seen such stark, primitive passion. They went at that dead beast like madmen, their knives flashing, their arms dripping blood. They yelled and sobbed with exertion as they tore at the hide and hacked out the flesh, thrusting dripping morsels into their mouths and flinging the chunks back to their women, who struggled on the storming outskirts."[25] In contrast, her description of Tanganyika's Watusi people was considerably more tolerant: "The Watusi are born aristocrats, tall and slender as wands—some of the men are seven feet and over—bronze skinned, with finely modeled hands and feet, and oval, clear-cut features, of an Egyptian cast."[26]

Mary Hastings Bradley's second African book, *Caravans and Cannibals* (1926), was met with the same enthusiasm from critics as her first. "Mrs. Bradley knows how to make you see and smell her 'Caravans and Cannibals,'" exclaimed a reviewer for the *New York Times*. "This woman explorer has shot all kinds of African game; and her book contains an interesting discussion of the peculiar traits of each."[27]

Mary and Herbert Bradley's last big game hunting trip abroad was in 1928 to India and Ceylon (Sri Lanka) to bag tigers and other game. Invariably, the couple arrived at shooting grounds in different venues at times when virtually no big game was to be found. Finally traveling to Sumatra (in Indonesia), they were invited to sit in a blind and wait for a marauding tiger to be lured to a slaughtered buffalo. Impatiently, Mrs. Bradley crouched in the blind, straining her eyes to catch a glimpse of their quarry. When a huge tiger suddenly seemed to materialize from the jungle shadows, she lifted her rifle and aimed at her target. "I never felt so cold and tense in my life," she recalled.[28] Though her shot was true, the tiger disappeared. Bradley left her blind and entered the dimly lit jungle. "The tiger was lying stretched out, about fifty yards away from the buffalo," she later wrote. "As we came up he roared with fury, dying as he was—dying by violence as he had lived. He had been terrible in life and he was terrible in death."[29] Her book recounting the trip, *Trailing the Tiger* (1929), was more of a travelogue than a hunting book when compared to her African works.

Bradley continued her writing career, this time teaming with daughter Alice as illustrator in both *Alice in Jungleland* (1927) and *Alice in Elephantland* (1929). Through the 1930s, she published a four-volume novelization of the history of Chicago, as well as a number of mystery novels. In 1931 and again in 1938, she received the prestigious O. Henry Award for best short stories. During World War II, she traveled to Europe as a correspondent and was one of the few Allied women present at the liberation of some of the infamous Nazi concentration camps. Her last novel was published in 1952. Mary Hastings Bradley died in 1976.

GRETCHEN CRON

Like Mary Bradley, Gretchen Cron shared a life of adventure with her husband. The daughter of a New York steamship-company executive, she had excelled in high school athletics, then was sent to a finishing school in Switzerland. A traveling companion to her father, she also acted as company secretary during World War I. After her father's death, she married Herman Cron, a German owner of hunting estates along the Rhine near Baden and in the depths of the Black Forest. She learned to hunt pheasant, woodcocks, waterfowl, and deer. The beauty of the forest retreat and her hunting stand among the trees made a profound impression on her:

> For hours I have clung to the branches of some great tree, peering anxiously along a faint trail below me, straining my eyes for the smallest stir in the foliage, or listening for the snapping of a twig. And finally at evening, with the lights of the distant villages twinkling like fireflies, I have watched till the last of the after-glow died in the west—and then have gone home without a glimpse of my quarry, but happy to have been able to hunt him in this enchanted wood.[30]

While hunting in Germany presented enjoyable aspects of sport, the Crons decided they needed greater challenges. Though they had made trips to Egypt, Norway, and the West Indies, they decided a real adventure would be hunting with rifle and camera in Kenya. Their trip in 1925 would be the first of four East African safaris chronicled in no particular order in Gretchen Cron's only book, *The Roaring Veldt* (1930).

Sailing from New York to London, the couple embarked by steamship for Mombasa on Kenya's coast. Their caravan consisted of native attendants, three trucks for supplies and personnel, and a car. Among the supplies were three tents, a dining tent, canvas bathtubs, folding cots (only for the white members of the safari), and air mattresses complete with bicycle pumps for inflation. Among their rifles were large caliber double rifles by Holland & Holland and Westley Richards and bolt-action Mannlicher rifles for smaller game.

Gretchen Cron did not want to draw any more attention to herself as a hunter, or have anyone consider her unfeminine, noting that "I do not want to be thought to claim credit for being a woman who was doing a man's work." She believed, however, that "any healthy woman with a love of sport can hunt through . . . Africa today almost, if not quite, as easily as a man."[31]

While on safaris in Kenya and Tanganyika, Cron and her husband experienced the hardships and dangers of the trail and the small luxuries of camp life. On one excursion, both Herman Cron and Hans, his wife's brother, were stricken with fever. Gretchen managed to nurse them as their column slowly wound its way through the jungle toward a settlement. While diseases and injuries presented difficulties, the comforts of a hot bath in collapsible, portable bathtubs was present as well. Water was heated in petrol tins placed next to the campfire. Though privacy was always an issue, Gretchen Cron recalled that there was usually enough brush about to hide the tubs from the "eyes of the camp." She noted the delight in taking off her high-laced hunting boots and voluminous Stetson, to bathe in hot water and then to "slip into a pair of clean pajamas and soft mosquito boots."[32]

The Crons also contended with native porters who not only were bored with camp life but also desired to return to their villages. Gretchen Cron believed that as a white woman in Africa, she had to exhibit patience, perseverance, and an aura of great knowledge to maintain her perception of her superiority over the porters. While waiting in her Kenyan camp for her husband to return from a day's shooting, she noticed that the porters had suddenly become agitated. Leaping and gyrating in dance, the Kenyans knew the woman was stealing glances at them, so their efforts continued with great energy. In bewilderment, Cron could only guess at what had caused the disturbance. "I didn't know what the trouble was, and to have asked a neutral native about it would have destroyed my prestige. I could only sit there and wonder what it was all about. They *knew* I could see it, and that probably I was watching it from time to time. And so they fairly outdid themselves. I knew that if I gave them the satisfaction of seeing I was aware of it, my stock would go way below par."[33]

During their safari into Tanganyika, Cron and her husband visited a Masai village. She noted with glee that the Masai never guessed her to be a woman until she had been in their camp for some time. "Seeing me in my khaki clothes, like Herman's, with my hair slicked back and tucked under my helmet, they never realized my sex ," she recalled, "then just to please them I would raise my helmet and let down my hair, while they crowded around staring and giggling like little children at a side-show." She also admitted that she did not like the natives to get too close to her because Masai "ideas of sanitation and cleanliness weren't exactly civilized."[34]

Many women hunters toted cameras on their sporting excursions. Photographic equipment of the day was still relatively cumbersome and awkward to handle, aside from small pocket cameras. Focusing and adjusting, snapping the shot or manually cranking a movie camera required concentration, and amateur photographers sometimes forgot the unpredictability of wild beasts. While photographing a lion, Gretchen Cron failed to realize how close the big cat had approached. With her legs dangling from the edge of the safari car, she kept working the camera mechanism as the lion eyed her legs. After the feline finally sauntered away into the tall grass, Herman Cron informed his wife that he had had a very small window of opportunity to use his rifle if the lion had decided to attack her.

While on their 1928 expedition into Kenya, Cron and her husband trailed a herd of elephants. After Herman dropped one pachyderm, the rest of the great beasts stampeded. Forgetting that her husband was in close proximity to the herd, Cron let her desire to bag an elephant overrule her better sense. As the herd thundered by, she fired both barrels of her rifle at one huge bull, then watched as it disappeared into the brush. When her husband reproached her that the roar of her gun had almost deafened him as her shots passed close by, she admitted that she was afraid she wouldn't have any further chances to collect such a trophy and that it had been "partly a reflex action under the stress of the moment."[35] Had her bull suddenly turned upon the shooters, he reminded her, it would have been disastrous with both elephant guns empty.

At the end of the months spent on the African veldt, and with the return to civilization approaching, Gretchen Cron revealed her uneasiness at shedding her beloved khakis and boots for more feminine dresses and footwear. Shoes in particular provided a degree of angst. "When I put on my light high-heeled shoes, after the heavy boots I had been wearing for weeks," she later wrote, "I felt as though I were walking on nothing but treacherous air currents that threatened to trip me with every step I took."[36]

While Cron alluded to a future hunting expedition to Indochina, no record of that excursion has been uncovered. *The Roaring Veldt* remains her only book, and as with other big game hunting works written by women, it received the condescending approval of critics as novelty adventure. A reviewer for the *Boston Transcript* noted that "there is a 'feminine' element in this book which gives it the novel appeal of a delectable incongruity."[37] At least one critic determined that Cron's effort was valuable as sporting or adventure literature without the novelty tag. Kermit Roosevelt, the son of former president Theodore Roosevelt and himself an experienced big game hunter, described the book "as a most readable account of present day safari life in East Africa. [Cron] has made four expeditions and is in a position to speak with authority."[38]

GRACE KING

A sense of adventure coupled with a love of sport also drew Grace King to Kenya in 1924 and 1927. Born Grace Watkins in a small southern Minnesota town in 1875, she was the heir to the Watkins Products fortune built by her liniment peddler father J. R. Watkins. In 1904 she married typewriter salesman Ernest L. King, who eventually became company president. Had Grace King been male, surmised one writer, "she undoubtedly would have been groomed to assume control of the Watkins Company, but in that day in age female executives were so rare as to be nearly unthinkable."[39] The Watkins firm continued to expand, though Ernest King ran into problems during Prohibition when it was determined the company's liniments contained too much alcohol. The couple built the Winona National & Savings Bank in Grace King's hometown in Minnesota, an institution still in business today.

A renowned marksman with a shotgun, Mrs. King had been trained as a child by Annie Oakley.[40] She participated in numerous state and national trapshooting competitions, winning major events in Atlantic City and Chicago and placing at the prestigious Grand National Tournament at Vandalia, Ohio. At one time she held the women's trapshooting record with a string of 186 consecutive targets broken.

The Kings had already hunted in Minnesota and other parts of North America when they decided to go on their first African safari, accompanied by their teenage son, Buddy, in 1924. A stickler for details, Grace King provided an analysis of proper hunting attire for the Kenyan game field. In terms of underclothing, she suggested that "underwear should be selected with the fact in mind that it will be washed but probably not ironed."[41] While thin woolen underwear was theoretically acceptable, she surmised there were those who would find it torturous to wear, including women. Though her husband preferred lightweight woolen trousers, King added that "a feminine member of the party would wail loudly about wearing wool in the tropics." She suggested that women bring three pairs of cotton khaki pants. In addition, she advised them to pack several pair of heavy silk or cotton stockings for camp wear, not to mention a few pairs of woolen socks since they absorbed moisture and provided padding for the feet of those not accustomed to walking long distances, then added that hunters shouldn't forget stretchers to keep the socks from shrinking after washing. When it came to boots, King preferred her heavy, hobnailed boots because they didn't rub her ankles. "No pains should be spared to obtain the best possible leather and absolute comfort," she warned. "Feminine ankles, unaccustomed to anything heavier than silk stockings, are sure to blister and to be uncomfortable in the hardening process. Her boots should be as high as possible."[42]

The ubiquitous African insect pests were also noted by King. Kenya's ant populations, for example, featured not only stinging types but those with noxious odors as well. While scrambling down a rocky embankment to bathe at a river's edge, King found a number of biting ants in her clothing which had to be "pulled off by main force." When gathering exotic blossoms on another occasion, she found her hands covered with ants. At one camp, a colony of large ant species was discovered near the tents. Within a few days, a disagreeable odor permeated the air. Despite numerous efforts to locate the source of the smell, King finally ordered the tent floor to be removed. Under the canvas was an extensive colony of the odor-producing ants. The ants disappeared after campfire ashes were spread over the nesting area. Interestingly, Mrs. King felt the ants to be a greater pest problem than mosquitoes, even though she recognized the dangers of contracting malaria. "To a resident of Minnesota, accustomed to clouds of mosquitoes, day and night," she noted, "the African mosquito would seem negligible."[43]

Writing of her African safari twenty years after Agnes Herbert, Grace King also evaluated the proper guns for big game hunting. She claimed that the "most satisfactory procedure is to buy [a rifle] in England and have just the right stock put on it" to fit a woman's physique.[44] King's personal rifle was a .465 Holland and Holland double-barrel weighing twelve pounds. She chose the .465 because it was big enough for all African game, and it was the heaviest weapon she could hold steadily and shoot accurately. King was quick to note, however, that her husband's rifle and that of their professional hunter and guide was a .470 caliber, and she feared that in the heat of the hunt, the cartridges of the similar .465 and .470s might become intermixed with disastrous results.

While Ernest King did the bulk of the hunting, Grace also proved herself with her rifle, bagging leopards, elephants and hippopotamuses. Perhaps her most dangerous episode was in stalking buffalo. After wounding one bull, she and her professional hunter followed its trail into heavy brush country. With the injured bovine in the middle of a protecting herd, neither she nor the hunter could locate the beast long enough for a finishing shot. After hours on the trail, and with the sun setting, King declared she was too spent to tramp the many miles back to camp. Dispatching a native runner to her husband to bring tents and food, the pair built a fire to spend the night. With the roar of lions and hyena yelps drawing near, there was fear that they would become the prey. Fortunately, Ernest King showed up with the supplies, and a camp was quickly erected. By the next morning, however, the wounded buffalo was found dead and partially devoured by hyenas. The hunters, however, procured the head as a trophy.

Upon the Kings' return to Minnesota, Grace King wrote *Hunting Big Game in Africa* (1926), privately printing and marketing the work. The proceeds were donated to the American Trapshooting Association, while the trophies of the hunt were displayed in the couple's Winona bank, where they are still on display. The Kings also planned a shooting expedition to French Indochina (Vietnam) for tiger, but a record of that journey has yet to be discovered. After the death of her husband, Grace King apparently gave up hunting. She died in 1975.

DIANA STRICKLAND

Unlike the big game hunting adventures of Grace King, Mary Hastings Bradley, and others who traveled with their husbands, Mrs. Diana Strickland led her own safari into the heart of the Belgian Congo. Her books reveal little of her early life, nor do they identify her husband. Leaving London in 1923, the woman commented that "it is an uplifting experience to find oneself in command of an expedition." She chose the Congo because she felt it was less explored and that "progress and development there has been more slow than in other parts, and the civilization which has been imposed on the native more crude and less transforming"—a reference to the rather heavy handed colonial rule of Belgium.[45] Though Strickland commanded the shooting party, three English male companions simply referred to as Briggs, Payn, and Douglas accompanied and hunted with her.

Clothing and cleanliness were concerns as Strickland and her companions entered the dank forests of the Congo. Echoing Grace King's advice, she considered footwear to be the most important item in a hunter's personal outfit. Depending on the type of terrain and climatic conditions in the hunting zone, she recommended high, waterproof canvas boots for swampy country, while "for shooting in thorny country high soft leather boots with crêpe soles, also plenty of comfortable shoes to be worn with stockings—this was one of the favourite forms of footgear in which we walked many hundreds of miles without mishap."[46]

Bathing was problematic. There is no reference to the expedition carrying portable tubs, so local lakes and rivers must have been utilized. While camped near one small lake, the party delighted in bathing twice daily. Strickland coyly noted that bathing suits consisted of little more than bath towels, and men and woman enjoyed the lake simultaneously. When the expedition's supply of tinned soap was exhausted, alternatives had to be used. After bagging a hippopotamus, her safari porters converted hippo fat into soap. "The component parts consist of the stump of the banana tree dried and powdered, then immersed and puddled in boiling hippo fat," she noted in her journal. "When the banana powder has been stirred up in the boiling fat after the manner of a Christmas pudding, which it mightily resembles upon completion, and has arrived at a certain consistency it is left to cool and then cut into tablets of the required size and stowed away in tins. Its cleansing qualities are really remarkable."[47] She warned, however, that while as a scouring medium the hippo soap should not be sniffed at, it also should not be sniffed up!

As Strickland's expedition wound its way into the rain forest, the party encountered a particularly dismal and remote region. Rather than entering a "second Eden," as she had expected from information garnered from books on the area, Strickland found a nightmarish course of swamps, downed trees, and interminable vineworks. At times her safari tramped nearly thirty miles to find a campsite free of ooze: "Dank, moist heat seemed to drape us like mantles, at times almost overwhelming. It would be a misnomer to speak of scenery through which we passed. What in reality obtained was steaming, dripping aisles of trees and vegetation, occasionally relieved by stretches of open ground mainly in the vicinity of the river bed."[48] Even Strickland's resolute character was affected by their slow pace, "hampered in our progress by horrible swamps and evil-smelling stretches of forest land, pregnant with disease and fever."[49]

Flying and crawling insects provided their own brand of horror for the woman. Strickland noted that at sunset, her camp was suddenly invaded by a dense cloud of mayflies. "The lamps particularly attracted them," she recalled, "and were speedily extinguished; the table was covered by them and our soup rendered uneatable. They proceeded to settle upon the tents like a black mantle and our beds were smothered with them."[50] In a similar vein, she was also introduced to the annelids of the Congo rain forest: "The common earth-worm of the forest attains an enormous size, some of them being as large as small snakes, about nine inches long. They are light blue in colour and at first inspired me with an unaccountable horror."[51]

Undoubtedly her worst encounter with insect life was through ticks carrying spirrilum fever. After being bitten, she described incredible bouts of weakness combined with excruciating pain to her back and head. After being delirious for many days, and craving water only to vomit blood after drinking, Strickland's temperature soared to 107 degrees. When her fever finally broke, she was able only to crawl on the floor of her tent. Her full recovery took months as her safari limped along.

Despite the difficulties of the terrain, climate, and insect infestations, she had traveled to the Congo to hunt big game. Though she did not note the genesis of her ability to handle a rifle and shoot accurately, she proved her familiarity and determination on numerous occasions. Having the right caliber rifle in hand often meant the difference between life and death. During one hunting episode, a wounded elephant charged her party. When the .470 rifle used by one of the other hunters jammed, Strickland swung her .375 Express bolt action to her shoulder and fired twice with little effect. With one cartridge left in the magazine, and with the enraged pachyderm bearing down on her companion, she waited until the beast had charged past her, then fired her remaining bullet. The elephant dropped. Up to that point on the safari, she had been using a

.303 rifle, which would not have had the penetrating or shocking power of the .375.

During an encounter with a bull buffalo, one of her hunting companions wounded the animal with his .470 rifle. Though badly hurt, the buffalo angrily sniffed the air, searching for its attackers. "We had had sufficient experience of these brutes to know that if it was wounded at all the position was one fraught with considerable danger," Strickland noted, "for a wounded buffalo is one of the most vengeful creatures of the wild."[52] Strickland's gun bearer fruitlessly emptied his rifle as the enraged beast charged. Her companion fired two more heavy rounds into the buffalo, while she delivered two rounds from her .375 Mannlicher. To her horror, the buffalo was within thirty feet of her companion when empty cartridge casings jammed his rifle. With one shot left in her bolt-action, Strickland side-stepped to get a better firing angle. The buffalo suddenly turned on her: "I stopped short and waited until it was about six feet off, my rifle raised ready in my hands. Then with a supreme effort I steadied my aim and fired straight between the eyes, and was lucky enough to pierce the brain with my last remaining bullet. It reared in the air and then fell with its nose only a few inches from my feet, stone-dead."[53]

Strickland and her companions struggled through the dripping rain forests, faced a brief mutiny among their native porters, and battled disease. As the expedition neared its end, she was invited to a dinner party given by a Belgian doctor in a Congolese town. Though she had a silk evening dress, she had no undergarment to wear. Planning to use a clean pair of khaki knickers as an underskirt, she was surprised to find the knickers missing from her tent. Deeming it inappropriate to wear the evening gown sans any type of lingerie, she substituted a white tablecloth. All went well at dinner, but when the party retired for coffee to the veranda of the doctor's home, Strickland suddenly found her tablecloth on the ground. "I stood petrified," she admitted. "The rest of the story needs no elaboration."[54]

Diana Strickland returned to London in 1924 and wrote a rather matter-of-fact account of the shooting trip based on her journal entries. Published the same year, her *Through the Belgian Congo* proved to be her only big game hunting book. An amateur entomologist, she had collected butterflies and other insects during the trip with the intent of writing a volume on Congolese insects, but apparently that project never materialized. Interestingly, her only other book was in an entirely different vein: *Love through the Ages* (1933) was an historical study of romance.

MARGUERITE MALLETT

Marguerite Mallett left England for Kenya in the waning days of World War I. There is little information on her earlier life provided in her book *A White Woman Among the Masai* (1923), nor on her motivations for sailing to Africa. After bouts with seasickness and a cryptic reference to her ship being stalked by a submarine, Mallett's vessel reached Mombasa via the Mediterranean Sea and the Suez Canal.

Mallett was quickly introduced to Kenya's insect population. During one journey into the jungle, her porters set up camp on a stretch of sandy soil. Once in bed, she lowered her lamp only to be set upon by hoards of beetles:

> Immediately something crawled across my forehead; I brushed it off and again closed my eyes. Then there was something in my ear; hurriedly I shook my head. Next a long-legged creature scurried across my lips. In disgust I turned up the lamp to see what the manner of beast was disturbing my rest. If one can imagine black ladybirds—that was exactly the size, shape, and general appearance of the beasts. They came in tens and twenties; they came in hundreds; they came in thousands, in battalions, in armies, in huge concourses; trillions would be but a few compared with the countless host that swarmed over the bed, covered my nightdress, and darkened the walls of the tent.[55]

Mallett also witnessed one of her pet dogs suddenly seized by a large python. With its coils winding tightly around the screaming canine, Mallett and her companion finally dispatched the reptile with numerous shots to the head. The close call kept her cognizant of the proliferation of reptiles in the region.

Traveling with friends into the interior, she recalled finding a jungle pool along the trail, its water "crystalline, you could count every pebble at the bottom."[56] Surrounded by tropical orchids and guarded by a huge fallen tree, she luxuriated in her bath but was well aware that the stream feeding the pool was the drinking place of leopards, lions, and a host of other game. On a subsequent visit to the bathing pool, she discovered a leopard preparing to spring perched in the trees above the water. With barely time to snap her rifle to her shoulder, Mallett managed to shoot the feline.

Mallett hunted a variety of antelope in the region, proving herself a sure shot. But her near encounter with a roaring lion at night left her numbed with fear. Every time the big cat roared, it sounded as if it were getting nearer. She had committed a cardinal error when she left her wagon, which had broken down, and proceeded to walk home along an unfamiliar path. As darkness and fatigue set in, she built a small fire and dispatched her native companion to bring help. Crouched near her little fire in the brush near the trail, with the lion's roar sounding nearer, she tried to rise but found her legs wouldn't support her. "I shivered from head to foot as the hideous roars reverberated and died away, only to be taken up and hurled back again," she recalled.[57] Fortunately for Mallett, natives showed up and brought her to her camp. The next night, the woman returned to the area with her hunting partner to bag the lion. Fires were lit around the camp. Suddenly the native porters shrieked as a lion sprang into the camp and turned with what appeared to be a man in its mouth. Mallett raised her rifle and fired: "The lion turned . . . crouching to spring . . . mane bristling, jaws distended, fangs glistening." She fired again and the lion, in a "rush of air, a swirl of dust," fell at her feet.[58] The "man" the feline had apparently seized turned out to only be a blanket. A shaken Mallett enjoyed the soothing effect of a tumbler of water and brandy.

Mallett spent considerable time among the Masai. Providing medical attention to the natives, she was at first horrified by their reactions to her ministering. The Masai would remove fresh bandages she had applied to burns and abscesses because the quality of the muslin she used was prized as cloth material. Once the ailing natives left camp, clean wrappings would be removed and soiled ones substituted. As for cleanliness, she noted, "to see me bathe the dirt off before applying treatment filled them with horror."[59] Mallett recorded her observations of Masai behavior in front of mirrors, examining her clothing and even watching her iron. With the natives having little knowledge of the outside world and contact only with British soldiers and sportsmen, Mallett concluded that in their minds, the Masai considered themselves "a degraded class of Englishman."[60]

During her trip to the region, Mallett was threatened by an insurrection of the Masai. She lost her notebooks and many photographs when her house was burned. During one tense episode, rumors of an impending Masai attack drove hundreds of other natives into the local British military camp. After the revolt was quelled, Mallett hoped that the Masai would recover and be schooled in the English tradition. She also hoped that native women would achieve a more equal status and that the "march of civilisation" would not "completely overwhelm this brave and fearless people."[61]

JOYCE BOYD

If Marguerite Mallett was vague in giving reasons for traveling to East Africa, Joyce Boyd was to the point: She and her husband raised cattle and crops on their sprawling ranch in Tanganyika. The vastness of the landscape, coupled with the remoteness of the farm impacted Boyd. "[We are] two little human ants and a few gray stones to shelter us, set down in this vast primeval jungle rolling away in unpeopled emptiness to seeming eternity," she soliloquized.[62]

Living in Africa meant Boyd had to be familiar with firearms to protect their herds from marauding leopards and lions and to hunt for sport. Some women worried about the resentments men might have for their incursion into a form of sport so seemingly masculine in nature. Joyce Boyd revealed the tension she felt when she hunted:

> I felt uncomfortably conscious of my sex. Men always rather resent women entering upon what they consider their particular fields of sport. I remembered frequent disparaging remarks I had heard men

> make in connection with women "big game shooting," and the nuisance they usually considered them to be. This was the greatest help to me now, for it had always made me indignant. Pride now demanded that, having entered man's field of sport, it was of the utmost importance to go through with it with as little trouble and nuisance as possible.[63]

The thought of stalking and being stalked by a leopard filled the woman with a combination of elation and dread. Boyd had departed her Tanganyikan farmstead armed with a double-barreled shotgun and a pair of buckshot loads to bag a bushbuck for the dinner table. On her path she discovered that the carcass of a calf had been dragged to an altogether different location, the sure mark that a predator was nearby. Boyd could hear grunting in the thick brush but was torn between bagging a beast that marauded her cattle herd and fleeing: "I was afraid. Undoubtedly I was. Very much afraid; in fact, I had never known what fear really was until this moment." Knowing her buckshot cartridges were effective only at close range, she imagined a tearing, rending fury of a leopard or lion arching toward her throat. Boyd battled what she perceived as her own cowardice: "I was a coward then, not even able to deceive myself. I should be forced to admit it in the future. Sick with fear and disgust at myself I made my decision." Suddenly a leopard appeared between her and the calf, "head down, teeth bared, tail viciously lashing from side to side, its yellow eyes fixed upon me, flaming with the light of killing." Nearly paralyzed with fright, Boyd squeezed the trigger of her shotgun, cognizant of the necessity of keeping the second barrel in reserve should the leopard spring at her. Badly hit, the feline dashed into the bush, grunting and snarling as it tore at the earth. With darkness setting in, Boyd backed away, then ran to her farm. Accompanied by her husband, she decided to track the wounded leopard the next day rather than venture into the shadows of the heavy brush. She spent a near sleepless night awaiting the dawn, imagining the trophy skin of the leopard stretched in front of her fireplace. In the morning, Boyd and her husband, with their Irish setters ranging into the bush, discovered the wounded leopard had made its escape.[64]

If she worried about her ability to bag game, she was also concerned about getting lost. Boyd admitted to the hysteria that could set in when losing one's bearings: "Once I got lost in the forest alone, shortly after I first came out to Africa. That is one of the things one never forgets. It is horrible. Ever since then that particular fear, a grim and ghastly companion, stalks ruthlessly beside me whenever I am alone in a forest, and a blind panic immediately takes possession of me." It was particularly trying for her when she would enter heavy jungle with towering trees and only "a patch of sky no bigger than a pocket handkerchief" to guide her.[65]

Other dangers in the wilderness were constantly present. While stalking a rhinoceros, Boyd was bitten in the shin by an unknown species of snake. Unable to face the rhino, she beat a hasty retreat, only to find her leg beginning to swell, noting that an "agonizing pain shot up my leg from foot to thigh as if a red-hot iron had been run up it." A three hour walk to camp turned into a five hour nightmare for the woman. Staggering over rocks and vegetation, her leg "was the size of a pumpkin and terribly heavy."[66] After stumbling deliriously into camp, she was fortunate to find out that only one reptilian fang had penetrated her leg. Phlebitis set in, and Boyd was bedridden for nearly three months.[67]

While Marguerite Mallett and Joyce Boyd wrote of their experiences from a similar venue, Mallett's work was poorly received by literary critics. The reviewer for the *New Statesman* noted that "we are not much enriched by this ill-written personal narrative."[68] The *Times [London] Literary Supplement*, also confused by Mallett's lack of focus, described the book as "puzzling . . . it is if a picture has been cut out of its frame irregularly and a little away from the edge."[69] The *Boston Transcript* admitted her manner of writing was straightforward "but not unusually entertaining."[70] Boyd, on the other hand, was praised for writing an unvarnished account of her adventures and was well received by the critics. The *New York Times* noted that Boyd's work was "an exciting, fascinating book, different from others that have come out of Africa, and very well worth reading both for its thrilling adventures and for the inherent interest of its story of life on an African farm."[71]

JULIE MORSE

"A funny little canvas tub" was how Julie Morse described her bathing apparatus while hunting on the Tanganyikan veldt. Born Julie Burke, she had married successful shoe merchant and big game hunter Ira H. Morse. When she accompanied him on her first safari to Africa in 1935, camp life, including the field bath, were new to her. She had porters fill the tub with one container each of hot and cold water, then would simply close her tent flaps and "perform ablutions in perfect seclusion and comfort. It's all great fun," she declared.[72]

Julie Morse discovered the dangers of being improperly prepared when hunting big game. After nearly emptying her .250 Savage lever-action rifle at a fleeing zebra, she finally bagged the animal, then discovered that her gun bearer had brought a bandoleer of .275 Mauser cartridges instead of the ammunition for her Savage. With only one .250 cartridge remaining, she guided her party back to camp. As they walked along the trail, a large lion suddenly appeared and stared at them. A startled Morse waited for the lion to move, noting that her "heart was doing handsprings from my throat to the pit of my tummy and back, and my arteries started to harden at that moment."[73] Fortunately the lion oozed peacefully into the tall grass bordering the trail.

The Morses made a number of trips to Africa and India to hunt big game and often included their son Philip on the expeditions. They opened the Morse Museum in Warren, New Hampshire, to house their trophies, artifacts, and curiosities collected on their journeys. In 1936 Ira and Julie Morse co-authored *Yankee in Africa,* which recounted Ira's earlier safaris and Julie's first trip. Her section, titled "Safari in the Rain," ably described the discomforts of African hunting during the rainy season. She subsequently contributed chapters to a series of pamphlets she wrote with her husband, which were sold at the Morse Museum.

NANÉ

As with the likes of Bettie Fleischmann Holmes, Grace King, and Gladys Harriman, a young English woman writing under the pseudonym Nané penned *Safari, The Diary of a Novice: Big Game Hunting in Tanganyika* (1937), a privately printed account of her big game hunting trip to Africa.[74] Joining her husband, Rhoddy (no last name given), and several other companions, the shooting party flew from London to Nairobi,

Kenya, with various stops in between. The days of safaris by steamer and overland caravan had seemingly come to an end by the late 1930s.

Nané's recounting of her adventure included the relative comforts of traveling by Ford truck to the hunting grounds, enjoying daily tea, and luxuriating in afternoon baths. A bit more worrisome for her was the makeshift latrine placed about twenty yards from the tents, surrounded by brushwood with a "narrow entrance, and in the centre, a wooden stool . . . standing over a deep hole in the ground."[75] In the literature of women big game hunters, it was one of the few mentions of toilet facilities.

As the safari proceeded toward the Ngorongoro Crater, a wide variety of game was collected. Nané bagged a lion, though she had been driven by truck into decent shooting range. Her misplaced first shot at rhinoceroses led her to bag a pair of the animals by accident. The rhino wounded by her initial shot disappeared into the brush. When she came upon a pair of rhinos a short time later, she bagged the larger with a single round, only to have the second animal fall as well. After examining the carcasses, it was determined the second rhino had finally succumbed to its wound from her first bullet at nearly the same time she had killed the other. The issue was problematic because the party had only one license for rhinoceroses.

Nané's account noted the frustrations of her first safari. She admitted to having difficulty climbing over trees and through heavy brush due to her short stature. While trucks delivered hunters to the shooting grounds, stalking required hours in the hot sun and over rough terrain which left her feeling stiff and fatigued. When she missed shots at game, she fretted that her luck had deserted her. As her safari came to an end and she and her husband packed for the return flight to London, she admitted that despite the physical discomforts, she was "hoping and praying" that she could return to "that wonderful open air life" and hunt elephants, leopards, sable antelope, and kudu.[76]

FLORENCE H. MORDEN

Noted explorer, scientist, and big game hunter William J. Morden wrote only one book concerning his expeditions to central Asia in the

1920s. While he penned many articles for various journals and conducted expeditions under the auspices of the American Museum of Natural History, little is mentioned in his writings of his first wife, Florence H. Morden, or of her trips abroad.

Florence Morden kept a detailed notebook of her personal experiences, as well as writing numerous letters and other correspondence for her husband. In 1922 she accompanied him on a trip to Kenya to collect a variety of big game. Camp life included native porters pulling off the hunters' heavy boots, filling portable bathtubs, and mixing a potent camp beverage known as a "Blue Niler." She described the porters as being "likable lads, a bit shy of us, but so willing to work hard, and so ready to do anything we want."[77]

Using a heavy .470 rifle, Morden bagged a leopard from inside a cave, then later missed a lion at close range, an episode that left her devastated. "My own failure utterly stunned me," she admitted in her notebook. "Wave upon wave of a sort of sick disappointment and rage passed over me." When the local natives found out that she had missed, she noted that "every place I looked, staring eyes from solemn black faces seemed to reproach me."[78] Ten days later, she managed to wound a big lion that was recovered later in the day. Her porters and local tribesmen hefted her to their shoulders with glee and paraded her around the camp as the lion, slung on a pole, was brought in. When confronting a charging lion on another occasion, she admitted that her knees "refused to behave as decent, respectable knees are supposed to behave, and shook disgracefully."[79]

In 1924 Florence and Bill Morden traveled to India, where they joined several British army officers for a tiger hunt in Nepal. On elephant back, the shooting party entered the scrub brush as native beaters drove the tigers to them. Florence Morden noted that the .470 rifle she had used in Africa was too big for safe use from an elephant's howdah. She switched to a shotgun firing solid, round balls and bagged a pair of tigers.

Morden was concerned with how she was being perceived as a sportsman. During her Kenyan hunt after elephants, after tense moments in the jungle with pachyderms nearby, she railed against her husband and their professional hunter for not letting her shoot. They had to remind her, she admitted, that it was not sporting to shoot an elephant with undersized ivory. On her Indian trip, she questioned the sporting aspect of shooting tigers from the safety of elephant back—then dismissed the philosophical concern by noting "the killing of a tiger is a public benefaction."[80]

Florence Morden traveled throughout northern India and into China in support of her husband's scientific expeditions. In the autumn of 1923, while William Morden was hunting Ovis ammon in central Asia, she and her sister journeyed on foot through western Tibet. By the late 1920s, with China ravaged by civil wars, she planned on traveling by train to meet her husband's expedition returning from months in the field. When Shanghai officials warned her that it was too dangerous for a white woman to travel such a distance by rail, she hired a Chinese houseboat to take her northward by sea, then embarked on a much shorter land journey. She arrived in Peking thirty-six hours before her husband.

Outside of a few magazine articles, Florence Morden did little writing recounting her adventures. After she died in April 1939, William Morden collected her notebooks and letters, privately publishing excerpts in a limited edition volume titled *From the Field Notebook of Florence H. Morden* (1940). His dedication simply read "These extracts, from the notebook that she kept, are dedicated to her memory."[81]

KATHLEEN GLOVER

Kathleen Glover's story is different in the sense that she related her adventures to English author Marjorie Hessell Tiltman, who included them in the third person in her compendium *Women in Modern Adventure* (1935). Glover, as noted by Tiltman, grew up in London, eschewing the fashionable shopping districts of the great city for the haunts of gunmakers' shops and private shooting ranges. As a young woman, she went on her first big game hunting expedition to Kenya.

After her marriage, she and her husband embarked on a combined exploratory and hunting trip to central Africa. In 1928 they arrived in Nigeria to enjoy the sport in the region, then proceeded inland. Near Lake Chad, Kathleen Glover encountered a rare albino bull elephant. After crouching and stalking the pachyderm along the edges of the lake, she stood up to gain a better shot. As the elephant charged, she suddenly lost her footing in the mud. She recovered her balance long enough to drop to one knee and fire a round. The raging bull plucked her from the mud with its trunk and flung her through the air. Moments later, after she recovered consciousness, she discovered her shot had penetrated the elephant's brain, killing it, though not before it had seized her. "It is these unexpected moments that add zest to the sport of big-game hunting," she later admitted in grand understatement to Tiltman.[82]

The Glover's journey through Africa presented greater dangers than just the attacks of wild animals. As their caravan approached a series of ravines and defiles, a band of men and camels among the ravines was detected. Suspecting bandits, the couple kept a watchful and apprehensive eye in that direction. When their guides suddenly bolted, the Glover's halted their column, ringing themselves and their porters with a wall made from their supplies. With the sun setting and the mounted bandits approaching, Kathleen Glover and her husband fired into the darkness to keep the cutthroats at bay. "Don't let them take you alive," warned her husband.[83] After a terror-wracked night, the couple viewed the rising sun with relief as the bandits finally galloped away.

Camp life also presented dangers. At one particular site, with her husband away, Kathleen Glover had been disturbed on successive nights by footsteps prowling around her tent. With revolver drawn, she left the enclosure to chase away two native men who had been skulking nearby. On a second night, the same drama was enacted again with the same result. By the third evening, the natives boldly entered her tent knowing there was no white man in camp. Glover was forced to fire her revolver, wounding one of the prowlers. It was later discovered that the natives were local thieves who would have cut her throat to get what they wanted.

In 1931 the Glovers embarked on an even more ambitious undertaking. With the backing of Shell Oil Company, they procured several International six-speed cars in an attempt to cross Africa by motor vehicle. During the 2,500-mile journey, the expedition met with incredible hardships. Supply depots of food and fuel proved to be too few. When roads disappeared into sand dunes, the running boards had to be stripped from the cars in order to proceed. The burning heat took its toll on humans and vehicles alike. At one point, Kathleen Glover became so weak from lack of water that she drank from the car radiators—and that after the water had been previously drained for washing purposes and then refilled into the radiators.

The Glovers returned to England, though Tiltman admitted that Mrs. Glover refused to talk about some of the horrors of the journey. The chapter in Tiltman's book apparently is the only record of Kathleen Glover's African adventures.

OLIVE SMYTHIES

When eighteen-year-old Olive Smythies decided to leave her home in Somerset in England to marry Evelyn Smythies, a recently appointed forest officer in India, it was with an admission that she was in love, and "it seemed a grand adventure to get away from my sheltered home and taste the wilds of the Indian jungle."[84] Her honeymoon in 1911 was brief as her husband announced he had to begin his tour of the Kumaon district in northern India. For the next thirty years, she shared his travels, hunted big game, and carried on a love affair with the country.

With her husband attending to his official duties for long periods of time, Olive Smythies was determined not to let boredom set in. Knitting and embroidery offered her few pleasures, and there was just a handful of books to read. "*Shikar,*" she later noted, "would afford a welcome relief from the monotony."[85] Preferring a lightweight .256 Mannlicher rifle, she was so excited on her first hunt after goral, a species of wild goat, that she could not hold her rifle steady and missed her target by many yards. By the time she finally bagged a goral, she discovered that she had climbed high into the mountains which left her trembling with fright—she was afraid of heights!

Sporting opportunities abounded for Smythies. She bagged deer and otters with her rifle, shot pheasant and partridges with a shotgun, and enjoyed angling for mahseer and other fish in India's rivers and streams. The couple also hosted numerous extravagant shooting parties with guests demanding the finest in cuisine and service.

In December 1925, she faced her greatest challenge. Positioned on machans fifteen feet off the ground, Smythies and her husband waited for tigers to come to their bait. She wounded a tiger with a hasty shot, then was horrified to see the enraged feline clawing its way up her tree to her machan. Backing away on the tiny platform, she jammed her rifle barrel into the tiger's mouth and pulled the trigger. The rifle misfired. As the beast's claws ripped apart the string seat of the machan in its endeavor to reach her, she fell backward, slamming into the ground. Though stunned, she scrambled to her feet expecting the tiger to be on her in a moment. Only after colliding with the earth did she realize her husband had managed a clear shot and killed the tiger. For years afterward, Olive Smythies would wake in the middle of the night screaming that a tiger was after her.

Though the tiger hunting episode was unsettling, the woman recovered and continued to hunt big game. Her favorite method of hunting was *ghooming*, riding through the jungle on elephant back and shooting "anything from a jungle cock to a tiger."[86] She and her husband played host to visiting European royalty bent on bagging all manner of game, hunted with an American group wanting to taste every species bagged (including vulture), and participated in a maharaja's hunt.

When Evelyn Smythies retired in 1940, the couple hoped to return to England. World War II interfered, however, so they settled in Nepal. On a subsequent trip to India, they discovered the violence erupting in countryside and city as the push toward Indian independence gained momentum. Evelyn Smythies barely eluded a mob that stopped the train he was traveling on. When Olive and her son were finally reunited with her husband, the family spent a terror-filled night in a bungalow as rioters searched for Europeans.

After the war, Olive visited her son in Burma, which was in the throes of its own independence movement. Stopping in Calcutta at the height of communal slaughter, she stayed at a friend's residence. During the night, she could hear tanks rumbling through the streets and a mob battling in a nearby bazaar. "It was the most terrifying sound I had ever heard and I could not sleep," she later noted. "As I lay awake I thought of the mere handful of Europeans in Calcutta compared to the hundreds of thousands of Indians."[87]

After returning to England, Olive Smythies wrote several books describing her life and adventures in India. Both *Tiger Lady* (1953) and *Ten Thousand Miles on Elephants* (1961) captured her big game hunting exploits. *Jungle Families* (1954) was a work of observation and life in India and Nepal.

LUCILLE PARSONS VANDERBILT

Perhaps the ultimate in champagne safaris was enjoyed by Lucille Parsons Vanderbilt. As newlyweds, she and her husband traveled by ocean-liner, train, and air to Egypt and Kenya in 1935. Luxury hotel rooms awaited her where available, as well as tailored safari suits and a brand-new rifle with three hundred cartridges. Besides the standard necessities of a hunt, her safari included an electric icebox, a generator of sorts, a Victrola, and plenty of liquor. A small plane kept in contact with the caravan, spotting wild game and winging in such niceties as ice cream hand-packed in Nairobi.

Motoring by a Dodge sedan and trucks into the interior, Lucy Vanderbilt admitted that the dust of the road left her feeling so dirty that even a bath with heated river water in a canvas tub appealed to her. She enjoyed camp life, though the trucks carrying her personal baggage got stuck in the mud, leaving her without a change of clothes for several days. "The worst inconvenience of all," she noted in a letter to her mother, "is the absence of a [toilet] tent or any toilet paper, and absolutely no way to get clean, and I am so muddy and dirty as you couldn't believe . . . I have no powder or lipstick."[88]

Armed with a new rifle, Lucy Vanderbilt proved to be an exceptional shot. She bagged several antelope, though the struggles of a wounded topi left her feeling ill. Trophy lion and buffalo also fell to her gun. While stalking rhinoceroses through thick brush in the Serengeti, she was shocked at how quickly a charging rhino could move. "He was coming straight at us, not ten yards away by now, and I aimed the gun and fired," she penned in another letter. "I was in such a state of excitement that I don't even remember taking time to aim, because when you see a great beast like that coming for you, you really get a scare."[89] Wounded, the rhino swerved away before being dropped by another hunter. Both Philip Percival and Bror Blixen, her professional hunters, admitted that she was both a good shot and a steady hunter in the field.

After her return to the United States, Vanderbilt collected the seventeen letters she had written to her parents and published them as *Safari. Some fun! Some fun!* (1936), a privately printed work limited to only fifty copies. Though the letters contained numerous spelling errors that were left intact in her publication, they also revealed an unvarnished account of a young woman proving herself on safari.

Numerous other women hunted big game in Africa and Asia in the post–Great War era, but their adventures are described in books written by husbands or other men. Colonel J. C. B. Statham, for instance, took his new bride on a sporting excursion in Africa, though he never named her in his book. Likewise, R. St. George Burke used both his and his wife's notes, as well as the experiences of his son and daughter, in writing of their Indian sporting trips in *Jungle Days, A Book of Big-Game Hunting* (1935). While Burke never mentioned his wife's name throughout the narrative, his daughter Norah Burke appeared as co-author on the title page.

Other women journeyed to Africa on safari but rarely hefted rifles. Mary Aline Buxton recounted her life in East Africa, but with her husband Clarence doing most of the hunting. Mrs. Patrick Ness noted in her book, *Ten Thousand Miles on Two Continents* (1929), that "once upon a time my husband and I planned a journey to British East Africa after big game," but there is no mention of her bagging game of any sort.[90] Likewise, Dorothy Una Ratcliffe, Margaret Carson, and Lavender Dower all wrote of their trips to Africa, but with husbands or other safari members doing the shooting.

While this book focuses on Anglo-American women, there are a few European women of note as well who hunted big game and wrote of their adventures. Perhaps the most famous was Danish-born Karen Blixen, who wrote under the pseudonym Isak Dinesen. Married to her cousin, famous big game hunter and womanizer Baron Bror Blixen-Finecke, she helped operate a large coffee plantation in the Ngong Hills in Kenya, an enterprise she maintained after her divorce in 1921. Her acclaimed book *Out of Africa* (1937) captured the beauty of the Kenyan landscape and the drama of African life in turbulent times. Though the book was not a hunting work per se, she included a lion hunt in her narrative, and noted that before she took over management of the coffee farm, she "had been keen on shooting and had been out on many safaris. But when I became a farmer I put away my rifles."[91]

Other Continental women who went big game hunting and penned their stories includes German Mrs. D. Cammenici, who described her hunt in East Africa in *Diana, Hubertus und Ich* (ca. 1930). Norwegian hunter Sonni Krag visited a friend's coffee plantation in East Africa, then proceeded to hunt rhinoceroses, lions, leopards, and other game, all ably noted in *Blandt Lover og Negrer í Afrikas Indre* (1931). Italian Countessa Norina Dolfin-Boldu traveled and hunted in grand style after elephants in the Sudan, and tigers, and buffalo in India, episodes she described in *Giornali di Carovana* (1934).

But the time of the champagne safaris was coming to an end. When the world again erupted in war in 1939, big game hunting expeditions came to a virtual standstill. Air and sea routes were far too hazardous to embark on a sporting vacation. From 1939 to 1950, there were virtually no books written by women on safari. During the decades of the 1950s through the 1980s, only a smattering of big game hunting works were penned by women, as many African and Asian countries suspended sport hunting while struggling through the throes of revolution and war after gaining independence. Internationally, women's rights movements continued to attract social and legislative attention, but it seemingly had become gauche to hunt animals for sport, then write about it. In the more than half century since the beginning of World War II, barely a dozen books recounting women's adventures in big game hunting were written.

NOTES

1. Mrs. E. L. King, *Hunting Big Game in Africa* (Winona, MN: none, 1926), p. 15.
2. Dennis Holman, *Inside Safari Hunting with Eric Rundgren* (London: W. H. Allen, 1969), pp. 40–43.
3. Holman, *Inside Safari Hunting with Eric Rundgren*, p. 250.
4. Mary Hastings Bradley, *Caravans and Cannibals* (New York: Appleton, 1926), p. 33.
5. Mary Hastings Bradley, *On the Gorilla Trail* (New York: Appleton, 1922), p. 80.
6. Mrs. Diana Strickland, *Through the Belgian Congo* (London: Hurst & Blackett, 1924), p. 14.
7. Osa Johnson, *Four Years in Paradise* (Garden City, NY: Garden City Publishing, 1941), p. 301.
8. Vivienne de Watteville, *Out in the Blue*, 2nd ed. (London: Methuen, 1937), p. 101.
9. de Watteville, *Out in the Blue*, p. 190.
10. de Watteville, *Out in the Blue*, p. 198.
11. de Watteville, *Out in the Blue*, p. vii.
12. Alice Bradley later married and became an award-winning science-fiction writer under the pseudonyms James Tiptree Jr. and Raccoona Sheldon.
13. Mary Hastings Bradley, *On the Gorilla Trail*, p. 7.
14. Bradley, *On the Gorilla Trail*, p. 86.
15. Bradley, *On the Gorilla Trail*, p. 65.
16. Bradley, *On the Gorilla Trail*, p. 263.
17. John Taylor, *African Rifles & Cartridges* (Georgetown, SC: Small Arms Technical Publishing Co., 1948), pp. 175–177.
18. Book review in the *Springfield Republican* (Jan. 28, 1923), p. 7a.
19. Mary Hastings Bradley, *Caravans and Cannibals*, p. 3.
20. Bradley, *Caravans and Cannibals*, p. 307.
21. Bradley, *Caravans and Cannibals*, p. 130.
22. Bradley, *Caravans and Cannibals*, p. 249.
23. Bradley, *Caravans and Cannibals*, p. 120.
24. Bradley, *Caravans and Cannibals*, p. 105.
25. Bradley, *Caravans and Cannibals*, p. 179.
26. Bradley, *Caravans and Cannibals*, p. 281.

27. Book review in the *New York Times* (Jan. 30, 1927), p. 7.

28. Mary Hastings Bradley, *Trailing the Tiger* (New York: Appleton, 1929), p. 214.

29. Bradley, *Trailing the Tiger*, p. 215.

30. Gretchen Cron, *The Roaring Veldt* (New York: G. P. Putnams, 1930), p. 15.

31. Cron, *The Roaring Veldt*, p. 59.

32. Cron, *The Roaring Veldt*, p. 192.

33. Cron, *The Roaring Veldt*, p. 96.

34. Cron, *The Roaring Veldt*, p. 155.

35. Cron, *The Roaring Veldt*, p. 65.

36. Cron, *The Roaring Veldt*, p. 283.

37. Book review in the *Boston Transcript* (March 15, 1930), p. 5.

38. Book review in the *Saturday Review of Literature*, vol. 6 (May 17, 1930), p. 1,045.

39. H. G. Hymes, "Winonan in Marksmen Hall of Fame," *Winona Sunday News Magazine* (June 9, 1968), p. 1.

40. Linda Mack, "Remnants of a Legend," *Minneapolis Star Tribune* (Oct. 22, 1994), p. 1E. Apparently King's father had hired Annie Oakley.

41. Mrs. E. L. King, *Hunting Big Game in Africa*, p. 75.

42. King, *Hunting Big Game in Africa*, p. 77.

43. King, *Hunting Big Game in Africa*, p. 259.

44. King, *Hunting Big Game in Africa*, p. 60.

45. Mrs. Diana Strickland, *Through the Belgian Congo*, p. 13.

46. Strickland, *Through the Belgian Congo*, pp. 14–15

47. Strickland, *Through the Belgian Congo*, pp. 160–161.

48. Strickland, *Through the Belgian Congo*, p. 92.

49. Strickland, *Through the Belgian Congo*, p. 94.

50. Strickland, *Through the Belgian Congo*, p. 172.

51. Strickland, *Through the Belgian Congo*, p. 172.

52. Strickland, *Through the Belgian Congo*, p. 221.

53. Strickland, *Through the Belgian Congo*, p. 222.

54. Strickland, *Through the Belgian Congo*, p. 275.

55. Marguerite Mallett, *A White Woman among the Masai* (New York: E.P. Dutton, 1923), p. 191.

56. Mallett, *A White Woman among the Masai*, p. 159.

57. Mallett, *A White Woman among the Masai*, p. 147.

58. Mallett, *A White Woman among the Masai*, p. 150.

59. Mallett, *A White Woman among the Masai*, p. 98.

60. Mallett, *A White Woman among the Masai*, p. 104.

61. Mallett, *A White Woman among the Masai*, p. 284.

62. Joyce Boyd, *My Farm in Lion Country* (New York: Frederick Stokes, 1933), p. 4.

63. Boyd, *My Farm in Lion Country*, p. 159.

64. Boyd, *My Farm in Lion Country*, pp. 30–42.

65. Boyd, *My Farm in Lion Country*, p. 151.

66. Boyd, *My Farm in Lion Country*, p. 154.

67. Boyd, *My Farm in Lion Country*, p. 158.

68. Book review in the *New Statesman*, 22 Supplement (Oct. 13, 1923), p. 12.

69. Book review in *The Times [London] Literary Supplement* (July 5, 1923), p. 499.

70. Book review in the *Boston Transcript* (Dec. 22, 1923), p. 2.

71. Book review in the *New York Times* (Sept. 24, 1933), p. 21.

72. I. H. Morse and Julie B. Morse, *Yankee in Africa* (Boston: The Stratford Co., 1936), p. 231.

73. I. H. and Julie B. Morse, *Yankee in Africa*, p. 242.

74. British antiquarian bookdealers R. E. & G. B. Way notes Nané's name as Mrs. Tennent in Catalogue 77.

75. Nané, *Safari, The Diary of a Novice: Big Game Hunting in Tanganyika* (no place: 1937), p. 12.

76. Nané, *Safari, The Diary of a Novice: Big Game Hunting in Tanganyika*, p. 80.

77. Florence H. Morden, *From the Field Notebook of Florence H. Morden* (Concord, NH: Rumford Press, 1940), p. 3.

78. Morden, *From the Field Notebook of Florence H. Morden*, p. 10.

79. Morden, *From the Field Notebook of Florence H. Morden*, p. 27.

80. Morden, *From the Field Notebook of Florence H. Morden*, p. 57.

81. Morden, *From the Field Notebook of Florence H. Morden*, dedication page.

82. Marjorie Hessell Tiltman, ed., *Women in Modern Adventure* (London: Harrap, 1935), p. 37.

83. Tiltman, *Women in Modern Adventure*, p. 46.

84. Olive Smythies, *Tiger Lady* (London: William Heinemann, 1953), p. 1.

85. Smythies, *Tiger Lady*, p. 8

86. Olive Smythies, *Ten Thousand Miles on Elephants* (London: Seeley Service & Co., 1961), p. 59.

87. Smythies, *Ten Thousand Miles on Elephants*, p. 163.

88. Lucille Parsons Vanderbilt, *Safari. Some Fun! Some Fun!* (Sands Point, NY: privately printed, 1936), p. 86.

89. Vanderbilt, *Some Fun! Some Fun!*, p. 100.

90. Mrs. Patrick Ness, *Ten Thousand Miles on Two Continents* (London: Methuen, 1929), p. 52.

91. Dinesen, Isak (Karen Blixen), *Out of Africa* (New York: Random House, 1938), p. 14.

NINE

With Arsenic, Rifle, and Camera: Delia Akeley and Osa Johnson

> "I believe there are few greater popular errors than the idea we have . . . that woman is a weakly creature. . . . It always seems to me that a hard-worked woman is better and happier for her work."[1]
>
> Francis Galton, 1872

Big game hunting was probably not on thirteen-year-old Delia Denning's mind when she ran away from her Wisconsin farm home in the late 1880s.[2] Nicknamed Micky, the boisterous young woman had a falling out with her parents over chores, discipline, and what she undoubtedly felt was the drudgery of farm life. Making her way to Milwaukee, the runaway met barber Arthur J. Reiss, and though she was only fourteen, the couple was married.

Little is known of Delia Denning's short-lived marriage to Reiss, and it is unclear how she met Milwaukee Public Museum taxidermist Carl E. Akeley. That she enjoyed assisting him in his private experiments with the art there is little doubt. By 1895, with a divorce from Reiss in her pocket, she followed Akeley to Chicago when he was appointed taxidermist for the Chicago Field Museum of Natural History. Denning and Akeley were wed on December 23, 1902.

Determined to study and collect wildlife to build more realistic museum presentations, Carl and Delia Akeley sailed for southern Kenya in 1905. By October they were collecting specimens near the Athi River. Garbed in a shooting jacket, long skirts, and a pith helmet, Delia Akeley soon learned of the difficulties of working in Africa. Rain and insects made life miserable. Elephant trails led through stretches of swamps and rotting vegetation. After game was bagged, the animals had to quickly be skinned before deterioration under the intense tropical sun began. Skins were rubbed briskly with arsenical soap and preservative salt, then bundled for shipping.

Delia Akeley also had to become familiar with rifles. Preferring a lightweight 6.5-millimeter Mannlicher-Schoenauer bolt-action rifle, she bagged an eland, her first head of African game, only to find out from her husband that the couple's hunting licenses did not include that species of antelope.

In 1909 Carl Akeley was commissioned by the Natural History Museum of New York to secure a family of elephants for a museum grouping. They were joined by *Chicago Tribune* cartoonist John McCutcheon in his baptism as a big game hunter.[3] In the Kenyan bush country, they met ex-president Teddy Roosevelt's expedition hunting and collecting game for the Smithsonian Institute.[4] Carl Akeley hunted with Roosevelt while Delia worked in camp at supervising the preservation of the specimens.

After McCutcheon left, the Akeleys turned their attention to the Kenyan highlands to collect elephants. Carl Akeley, however, fell critically ill, his wife admitting that "there were days and nights without cessation when meningitis, spirillum, and black-water fever, in turn threatened his life, that I did not close my eyes."[5] During the slow recovery period, Carl and Delia Akeley entered the forests near Mt. Kenia to bag elephants for the museum. As they approached a pair of bull elephants, they passed a solitary, apparently abandoned, hut. Carl, who was still suffering from the effects of fever, was slow in drawing a bead on one of the pachyderms. When he finally fired, the elephant, wounded, veered toward Delia Akeley "with terrific speed, screaming like a siren." Suddenly something touched her leg. A child carrying a baby had emerged from the hut and was also in the path of the enraged leviathan. "For a second I was petrified with horror," recalled Delia Akeley, "and then, with but one thought in my mind, I gripped my gun and pulled the trigger." The elephant collapsed ten feet from the hut.[6]

A particularly grisly death was in store for one of Delia Akeley's porters. When her husband had shot a large crocodile sunning itself on an island, two of the porters jumped into the river to swim to the island and retrieve the reptile for a hoped-for reward. The stronger of the two swimmers reached the island without incident, but the other did not. Though Carl Akeley had tried to provide rifle fire against other crocodiles swimming near, Delia Akeley saw the native "throw up his hands, clutch wildly at the air, and with a haunting, blood-curdling shriek that ended in a gurgle, disappear beneath the water."[7] Despite the efforts of firing more shots and throwing rocks in an attempt to get the beast to release his prey, the Akeleys realized they were helpless. As for the other porter who had reached the island, he used the dead crocodile as a raft and swam to safety.

On that same expedition, Carl Akeley almost lost his life in another way as well. Having left his camp and wife behind, he trekked into the forests to hunt elephants. After several days, two of the native guides returned to camp to report that Akeley had been attacked by an elephant. In the tropics, heavy rainfalls turned jungle trails to quagmires and often made them impassable. As the news sank in, Delia Akeley struggled to patch together a rescue party only to find the porters belligerent and about to desert. Fearing evil spirits and nighttime travel, they intended to kill her and leave her body for hyenas. Akeley confronted the porters, ridiculing and threatening them. When she finally got them to move, she found that two guides who had been with her husband had deserted. Through an awful night of lashing rain and powerful winds, she managed to locate the guides and secure them. Running back along a jungle path to the porters, she was suddenly attacked. As her coat was ripped away, she struck her attacker with her rifle butt, then raced through the storm to regather her relief column.

A nightmare of rain, wind, and lightning lashed the woman's relief party. Barely able to see, they plunged through the jungle:

> The tough, rope-like lianas and thorny creepers that hung down from the limbs of trees looped across the trail were like cold clammy hands, and caught us round the head and body, and in the dark tore our flesh in a painful way. We had to cross mountain torrents where the rushing volume of icy water nearly swept us off our feet. There were swampy patches, too, where the elephants in passing had left holes three and four feet deep in the soft, muddy ground. These swampy patches are difficult even in the daytime, but in the dark they are a hideous nightmare. The barefooted men crossed safely, but my hobnailed boots were a disadvantage. Three times what I thought was solid ground gave way, and I slid to the bottom of a hole with mud and water up to my waist.[8]

To make matters worse, a herd of elephants appeared on the trail ahead of the rescue party. Delia Akeley and her porters could hear the crashing of the great bodies ploughing through the trees and brush. When her porters panicked, she stood her ground, though admitting more from fear than personal courage. After what seemed an eternity, the elephants moved away and the rescue mission continued.

By morning the storm had dissipated, but her guides were lost. The resourceful Akeley fired rifle shots, answered by her husband's gun in the distance, until she located him. Carl Akeley had been mauled by an elephant that had pinned him to the ground between its tusks. Evidently the tusks had encountered some underground obstacle and had not penetrated too deeply into the soil, thus preventing the animal from crushing him. After his rescue, which she led once more through the jungle, she complemented the natives on "their final courage in braving both beasts and evil spirits in the jungle night."[9] It would take Carl Akeley months to recover from broken ribs and other injuries.

The Akeleys returned to the United States as heroes. While Carl Akeley plunged into his museum work, Delia became reclusive, remaining for months on end in their Manhattan apartment, almost completely absorbed in J. T., a small monkey brought back from Africa. The primate seemed to virtually control the woman's life, inflicting serious wounds on her leg and wrist, and ravaging the couple's apartment. Delia's absorption with J. T. became a symptom in the breakdown of the Akeleys' marriage. Perhaps the loneliness and stress she had faced in Africa had crumbled that bond. Carl Akeley's obsession with completing his museum work despite debilitating illnesses, which caused her considerable anxiety, may have contributed as well. When American troops were sent to Europe in 1918, Delia Akeley followed to work in military canteens in France. She remained in Europe until 1919, lecturing troops about her big game hunting adventures. When she finally returned, Carl Akeley moved to rooms at the Explorers' Club. In 1923 he filed for divorce, claiming that Delia had deserted him when she had left for France. She countersued on the grounds of desertion and cruelty, and a divorce was granted to her.

By that time Carl Akeley had met Mary Lee Jobe, and they were married in 1924. The newlyweds made a subsequent trip to Africa to collect gorillas for a museum exhibition. During that expedition, Carl Akeley died. Mary Jobe Akeley penned numerous books recounting the deeds of her famous husband (though she was only married to him a short time) and included her own adventures as well. Curiously, none of her books mentioned the role Delia Akeley had played in saving Carl's life decades earlier. Indeed Delia never appeared in the rescue passage at all; credit was given to one of the native guides instead.[10]

Even as Carl Akeley and Mary Jobe were being married, Delia Akeley embarked on her most daring expedition—a solo trip accompanied only by native porters and guides to collect gorillas in the Belgian Congo. For the next year, she tramped through the African jungles hunting and collecting specimens. The journey was fraught with discomfort, loneliness, and illness.

Though she had been exposed to Africa's vermin in earlier trips, the humid jungles of the Congo seemed to offer particular agonies. While traveling with members of a native tribe, she floundered through a thick ooze of mud, disturbing "millions upon millions of mosquitoes and tiny black flies." Surprised by the resounding hum of the insect legions, she struggled to maintain her balance. "My face and neck and hands and arms were so completely covered with the poisonous pests that no one could have told whether I was white or black," she later wrote.[11]

Rats became a plague for the woman as well as she rested in a native hut in the Congo. She could hear the rodents scurrying from their nests in the roof of the structure and crawling along the beams. What was worse, in her experience, was when the rats descended to the floor: "Sometimes the ugly, loathsome creatures would come close to my bed and standing upright sniff the air. The boldest would crawl up the legs of my cot, and once one of them leaped from the chair at the head of my bed and clung to my mosquito net until I struck it with my revolver and knocked it to the ground."[12]

As she passed through the depths of the Congo rain forest, Delia Akeley found herself the center of the natives' attention, particularly among the women: "After exclaiming over the color and straightness of my hair, examining my clothing, and slyly passing their hands over my breasts, they invariably asked about my family." She explained that though she was married, she had no children. To her chagrin, she found the natives suddenly disinterested. Finally understanding that the size of the family elevated the prestige of a woman, Akeley "decided to adopt a mythical family, and the next time I was asked the embarrassing question I boldly counted five on my fingers and then indicated their heights with my hand."[13]

Akeley continued on her journey, though she was ravaged by ptomaine and fevers. She spent time with a tribe of pygmies and was forced to combat mutinous porters. By the time she returned to the United States eleven months later, the woman had lost thirty pounds.

Delia Akeley penned a number of articles regarding her adventures and two books. "*J. T., Jr.*" (1929), her first book, recounted her and Carl's life with their pet monkey. *Jungle Portraits* (1930) provided descriptions of her early expeditions with her husband and her later solo trip to Africa. Though she planned a third book about her 1929 return to the Congo to further study pygmy life, none was forthcoming. In 1939 she remarried and reestablished contact with her family. Delia Akeley died in 1970.

While Delia Akeley had journeyed with her husband to Africa to collect museum specimens, Osa Johnson traveled with her spouse to that continent to photograph big game animals.[14] Born Osa Leighty in rural

Kansas in 1894, she was still in high school when she met and married Martin Johnson, photographer and traveling companion to Jack London. In 1917 she sailed with him to the Solomon Islands and Borneo to film the primitive tribes in the region, despite warnings from local authorities that some island populations were considered extremely dangerous. While she was in the New Hebrides, a local chieftain tried to claim Osa. In a heart-pounding chase through the jungle, both Osa and Martin were chased by tribesmen, barely making an escape to their whaleboat with their cameras and film miraculously intact. On trips to other islands, they discovered headhunters and cannibals. Upon their return to America, they produced their first film: *Among the Cannibal Isles of the South Seas*.

In 1921 Martin Johnson joined the Explorers' Club and met Carl Akeley. The venerable African traveler suggested that the Johnsons travel to East Africa to film wild game. With movie cameras in tow, the couple proceeded into the African interior, a venue where they would not only work but eventually take up residence. Though they had carried Jack London's Marlin .30-30 rifle to Borneo, both were unfamiliar with the dangers presented by Africa's big game and the necessity to be skilled with a rifle. Professional hunter A. Blayney Percival warned them that if they didn't learn how to hunt, the cost of hiring a professional to bag game to feed their expedition was likely to run $1,000 per month. The disconsolate Johnsons, already on a tight budget, realized they had to hone their shooting skills quickly. In their first attempt after game to feed the porters, Osa's gun bearer "showed clearly that he wasn't in the least honored to carry my gun," as she later recalled. After several failed attempts to bag antelope, the discouraged hunters returned to camp. Osa noted the gun bearers looking very sad, and that in their minds a gun bearer is "only as great as his white *bwana* (master) and that if a white hunter fails to live up to a certain standard, then his servant in turn becomes the laughing stock of his fellows."[15] The Johnsons' stock as hunters plummeted even farther when one of the gun bearers, an experienced fellow who had served on President Teddy Roosevelt's famous expedition of 1909, asked to use a rifle to kill some meat for the hungry porters. Osa finally proved her mettle when she downed two charging buffalo and a large leopard. "Our boys sang and danced with joy," she noted in her journal. "The *bwana* and *bibi* (mistress) were becoming real hunters."[16]

Osa Johnson had already been exposed to the discomforts of life and travel in the tropical regions of the Pacific, but Africa offered its own insect infestations. On one early occasion, she discovered a scorpion had entered her canvas tub as she soaked in a bath. From that time on, she made it a point not only to inspect her tub but also to always shake out her clothing and boots before putting them on lest scorpions had found a cozy place to nest. Upon retiring for the evening at one campsite, she experienced a veritable flood of insects and assorted other creatures into her tent. Rhinoceros beetles swept in kamikaze flights into the flame of her Coleman lantern, followed by flying ants. Toads hopped about, feasting on the dead insects, followed by a scorpion. Johnson and husband Martin watched the "picture of our Africa in action, with everything seeming to eat everything else." A tide of safari ants, which Osa likened to a "stream of black oil," seemed to flow into the tent, loading itself with the wings and carcasses of insects. The scuttling, crawling, writhing mass only continued to swell:

> Meanwhile more scorpions had moved in, some gold and others black, with red nippers like a lobster's, and the toads and other pests kept out of the way of their sharp and deadly tails. Sausage flies, dragon flies, hunting spiders, tiger beetles, crickets, praying mantis, spiders and ground-beetles of many colors were arriving; centipedes and six-inch worms, with as many legs as a centipede, one variety a light sand color and the other variety black; tarantulas, and finally a night adder about a foot long. The adder swallowed one of the toads, and I shut my eyes as I felt my stomach turn over.[17]

Osa called for the camp porters who came running. They killed the snake, fumigated the tent and swept out the debris of insect carcasses. Her experience was compounded by a night of terrifying dreams in which she faced "scorpions the size of elephants and toads with rhino bodies and safari ants as big as aeroplanes pushing me around. I shot them with my .470, but more came on for every one I dropped, and I woke up before dawn, wet as a rag and utterly exhausted."[18]

Osa Johnson often carried a heavy rifle when accompanying her husband on his motion-picture outings. Martin, the more accomplished with the camera, would usually maneuver to very close range to get his footage.

Osa, in the meantime, stood ready with her rifle if the animal attacked. That shooting wild animals at close quarters with a camera was worrisome for the woman was evident: "Sometimes, when Martin took the chances he did in getting much too close to elephants with his cameras, I wondered if he hadn't forgotten that he wasn't in a zoo and that there wasn't anything to protect him from being crushed to a pulp, except luck and the chance that I would shoot straight if the animals charged."[19] On one occasion, Martin Johnson disturbed a herd of elephants. With one massive bull chasing him, Osa continued to crank the camera, even though she realized his danger: "I kept screaming too, and my gun-bearer stood ready at my side with my rifle. Terror then was added to terror as the rest of the herd tore after the leader. One part of my brain told me that this would be a magnificent picture, the other told me that unless I brought the lead elephant down, Martin would be trampled." Seizing her rifle, Osa Johnson fired. The lead bull faltered and finally fell fifteen feet from where she stood.[20]

Osa and her husband discovered a secluded volcanic lake they dubbed Lake Paradise. For months they filmed and hunted game. Upon their return to the United States, more feature and short films were released. In 1923 they returned to Lake Paradise with a generous promise of $10,000 from Kodak camera mogul George Eastman. With supplies and materials packed into ten motorized vehicles, they proceeded back to Lake Paradise and built a bungalow complete with Osa Johnson's choice of frills. From that headquarters, they traveled through the region with cameras and rifles ready.

While Osa Johnson was experiencing a changing Africa, she was also introduced to a link with the continent's sordid past. During a buffalo hunting trip in northern Kenya, Osa Johnson's safari suddenly met a well-armed column of Abyssinians. The leader of the native party was grandiosely identified as the Habash of Abyssinia. After being assured that Osa was an American and not English, he invited her to sit and speak with him. He examined her expedition's cameras, guns, and even her fly-swatter of white colobus monkey fur. The Habash also questioned her as to her fears of being in unknown regions, and that "it is not usual to find a woman on safari by herself."[21] After a brief photo session and pleasant good-byes, Osa departed. A week later, she discovered the Habash was a notorious poacher and slave raider, only recently having attacked a native village where men were killed and women and children sold into slavery.

So renowned had the Johnsons become as moviemakers and hunters that they became the focal point of numerous sporting expeditions. In 1925 the couple served as hosts to the Duke and Duchess of York on their hunting trip. Osa, outfitted in her finest white silk shirt and tie and recently waxed car, promptly stuck the vehicle in a flooded stream bed and had to be hauled out by rope with the royal couple watching. A year later, George Eastman's safari hunted with the Johnsons, Eastman splitting his time between filming, shooting game, and helping Osa in the kitchen.[22] In 1927, after a special Boy Scouts of America drawing, three Scouts spent part of their summer hunting with the filmmakers.[23]

Throughout the 1920s and 1930s, Osa and Martin Johnson continued to produce movies of African wildlife and indigenous peoples including pygmies from the Congo's Ituri Forest. Martin Johnson penned a series of popular books recounting their travels and adventures. In 1932, as a concession to a modern era of flight, the couple purchased a pair of Sikorsky amphibious airplanes decorated in giraffe spots and zebra stripes to more quickly fly to shooting locales. Dubbed *Osa's Ark,* the zebra-striped plane contained photographic and sound equipment, a typing desk, and a tiny kitchen. The giraffe-spotted *Spirit of Africa* carried supplies and passengers. Both aircraft ferried the Johnsons and clients to a variety of locales. During one flight, Osa calculated that they had flown the distance in ten hours compared to the seventeen days of travel with George Eastman a few years earlier.

But the years of being virtually illness- and injury-free in Africa caught up to Osa Johnson. Stricken by pneumonia and fever, she nearly perished. An ice machine from Nairobi was brought to the mission hospital where she suffered through bouts of fever. After a shaky convalescence, the Johnsons returned to the United States, where Osa had surgery. There she learned her father had died. After recovering from the surgery, Osa and Martin decided it was time for a change of venue—they opted to travel and film in northern Borneo. For the next fourteen months, they prowled the jungle on foot and soared above it in their aircraft snapping pictures and cranking their movie cameras.

The Johnsons' final trip to the United States ended in disaster. In January 1937 the chartered plane they were using in flight to Burbank, California, crashed. Martin Johnson was killed, and Osa badly injured. Though her recovery was slow, she returned to Africa to supervise the filming of the Twentieth Century–Fox production of *Stanley and Livingstone* (1939). She also remained active by writing books and traveling on the lecture circuit. She penned two dozen articles for *Good Housekeeping* magazine, as well as articles for other periodicals. Her first book, *Osa Johnson's Jungle Friends* (1939), was written for young readers. In 1940 she published *I Married Adventure*, an autobiographical narrative of her life and adventures with her husband. The book became a best-seller and led to the publication of *Four Years in Paradise* (1941), which recounted the couple's earlier adventures near Lake Paradise.

In 1941 Osa Johnson married Clark H. Getts, her lecture tour manager. She continued to write articles and penned several animal books for children. Her *Bride in the Solomons* (1944) captured her adventures in the South Pacific as a newlywed decades earlier. Another manuscript describing her and Martin's 1935 journey to Borneo was discovered and published in 1966. Osa was preparing for a return trip to Africa when she died in her hotel room in New York in 1953.

Perhaps the most fitting epitaph for Osa Johnson was written by her husband and appeared on the dust jacket of *I Married Adventure*: "For bravery and steadiness and endurance, Osa is the equal of any man I ever saw. She is a woman through and through. There is nothing 'mannish' about her. Yet as a comrade in the wilderness she is better than any man I ever saw."[24] Such a final tribute easily fits many, if not all, women big game hunters.

NOTES

1. Francis Galton, *The Art of Travel (1872)* (Harrisburg: Stackpole Books, 1971), p. 8.

2. For additional biographical information, see Elizabeth Fagg Olds, *Women of the Four Winds* (Boston: Houghton Mifflin, 1985); Marion Tinling,

Women into the Unknown (Westport, CT: Greenwood, 1989). Both authors provide additional biographical and bibliographical information.

3. John McCutcheon, *In Africa: Hunting Adventures in the Big Game Country* (Indianapolis: Bobbs Merrill, 1910). McCutcheon notes Mrs. Akeley's presence a number of times and includes photographs of her.

4. Theodore Roosevelt, *African Game Trails* (New York: Charles Scribners' Sons, 1910). There are a few instances of meeting Mrs. Akeley in the Akeley camp.

5. Delia Akeley, *Jungle Portraits* (New York: Macmillan, 1930), p. 84.

6. Akeley, *Jungle Portraits*, p. 94.

7. Akeley, *Jungle Portraits*, p. 132.

8. Akeley, *Jungle Portraits*, p. 245.

9. Akeley, *Jungle Portraits*, p. 251.

10. No mention of Delia Akeley and her role in saving Carl Akeley's life is found in Carl Akeley and Mary L. Jobe Akeley, *Adventures in the African Jungle* (New York: Dodd, Mead and Co., 1930); Carl Akeley and Mary L. Jobe Akeley, *Lions, Gorillas and Their Neighbors* (New York: Dodd, Mead and Co., 1932); or Mary L. Jobe Akeley, *The Wilderness Lives Again; Carl Akeley and the Great Adventure* (New York: Dodd, Mead and Co., 1940). All these books were published after Carl Akeley's death.

11. Delia Akeley, *Jungle Portraits*, p. 218.

12. Akeley, *Jungle Portraits*, p. 105.

13. Akeley, *Jungle Portraits*, p. 174.

14. Tinling, *Women into the Field*. Tinling provides additional biographical and bibliographical information.

15. Osa Johnson, *I Married Adventure* (Philadelphia: J. B. Lippincott, 1940), p. 214.

16. Johnson, *I Married Adventure*, p. 233.

17. Osa Johnson, *Four Years in Paradise* (Garden City, NY: Garden City Publishing, 1941), p. 318.

18. Johnson, *Four Years in Paradise*, p. 318.

19. Johnson, *Four Years in Paradise*, p. 138.

20. Johnson, *I Married Adventure*, p. 288.

21. Johnson, *Four Years in Paradise*, p. 324.

22. George Eastman, *Chronicles of an African Trip* (Rochester, NY: John P. Smith, 1927). Eastman treated Osa Johnson like a daughter throughout his safari.

23. Robert Dick Douglas, Jr., David R. Martin, Jr., Douglas L. Oliver, *Three Boy Scouts in Africa: On Safari with Martin Johnson* (New York: G. P. Putnams, 1928). The authors are the three Boy Scouts.

24. Johnson, *I Married Adventure*, rear dust jacket panel.

Bibliography

PRIMARY SOURCES

Akeley, Carl, and Mary Jobe Akeley. *Adventures in the African Jungle*. New York: Dodd, Mead & Co., 1930.

——. *Lions, Gorillas and Their Neighbors*. New York: Dodd, Mead & Co., 1932.

Akeley, Delia J. *Jungle Portraits*. New York: The Macmillan Company, 1930.

Akeley, Mary Jobe. *The Wilderness Lives Again: Carl Akeley and the Great Adventure*. New York: Dodd, Mead & Co., 1940.

Baillie, Mrs. W. W. *Days and Nights of Shikar*. London: John Lane, 1921.

Baker, Florence. *Morning Star: Florence Baker's Diary of the Expedition to Put Down the Slave Trade on the Nile, 1870–73*. Edited by Ann Baker. London: William Kimber, 1972.

Bedford, Duchess of. "Ladies in the Field." In Henry Sharp. *Modern Sporting Gunnery*. London: Simpkin, Marshall, Hamilton, Kent & Co., 1906.

Blixen-Finecke, Bror von. *African Hunter*. Translated by F. H. Lyon. New York: Alfred A. Knopf, 1938.

Borden, Courtney (Mrs. John Borden). *Adventures in a Man's World: The Initiation of a Sportsman's Wife*. New York: The Macmillan Company, 1933.

Borden, John. *Log of the Auxiliary Schooner Yacht Northern Light, Commanded by John Borden . . . Borden-Field Museum Alaska-Arctic Expedition, 1927.* Chicago: privately printed, 1929.

Borden, Mrs. John. *The Cruise of the Northern Light: Explorations and Hunting in the Alaskan and Siberian Arctic.* New York: The Macmillan Company, 1928.

Bovet, Louis A., Jr. *Moose Hunting in Alaska, Wyoming, and Yukon Territory.* Philadelphia: Dorrance & Company, Inc., 1933.

Bovet, Mabel Morgan. "My Initiation to Big-Game Hunting." In Louis A. Bovet Jr. *Moose Hunting in Alaska, Wyoming, and Yukon Territory*, 88–92. Philadelphia: Dorrance & Company, Inc., 1933.

Boyd, Joyce. *My Farm in Lion Country.* New York: Frederick Stokes, 1933.

Bradley, Mary Hastings. *Caravans and Cannibals.* New York: D. Appleton and Company, 1926.

——. *On the Gorilla Trail.* New York: D. Appleton and Company, 1922.

——. *Trailing the Tiger.* New York: D. Appleton and Company, 1929.

Brooks, Virginia. *Screed of a Safari Scribe.* No place: privately printed, 1947.

Brown, Delores Cline. *Yukon Trophy Trails.* Sidney, BC: Gray's Publishing Ltd., 1971.

Bulpett, C. W. L. *A Picnic Party in Wildest Africa: Being a Sketch of a Winter's Trip to Some of the Unknown Waters of the Upper Nile.* London: Edward Arnold, 1907.

Burke, R. St. G., and Norah. *Jungle Days: A Book of Big-Game Hunting.* London: Stanley Paul & Co., 1935.

Burke, W. S. *The Indian Field Shikar Book,* 4th edition. Calcutta: "The Indian Field" Office, 1908.

Buxton, M. Aline. *Kenya Days.* London: Edward Arnold, 1927.

Caminneci, D. *Diana, Hubertus und Ich.* Berlin: no publisher, 1930.

Clark, James L. *Good Hunting: Fifty Years of Collecting and Preparing Habitat Group for the American Museum.* Norman: University of Oklahoma Press, 1966.

Coffrey, Leora S. *Wilds of Alaska Big Game Hunting.* New York: Vantage Press, 1963.

Colville, Mrs. Arthur. *1,000 Miles in a Machilla: Travel and Sport in Nyasaland, Angoniland, & Rhodesia, with Some Account of the Resources of these Countries; & Chapters on Sport by Colon Colville.* London: Walter Scott Publishing Co., 1911.

Crawford, Florence. *Girl of the Desert.* New York: Greenwich Book Publishers, 1961.

Cron, Gretchen. *The Roaring Veldt*. New York: G. P. Putnam's Sons, 1930.

Darrah, Henry Zouch. *Sport in the Highlands of Kashmir*. London: Rowland Ward, Limited, 1898.

Davidson, Lilias Campbell. *Hints to Lady Travellers at Home and Abroad*. London: Iliffe and Son, 1889.

Demidoff, E. *After Wild Sheep in the Altai and Mongolia*. London: Rowland Ward, Limited, 1900.

——. *A Shooting Trip to Kamchatka*. London: Rowland Ward, Limited, 1904.

De Watteville, Vivienne. *Out in the Blue,* 2nd edition. London: Methuen & Co., 1937.

Dinesen, Isak (Karen Blixen). *Out of Africa*. New York: Random House, 1938.

Dixie, Lady Florence. *Across Patagonia*. New York: R. Worthington, 1881.

——. *In the Land of Misfortune*. London: Richard Bentley, 1882.

——. *The Horrors of Sport,* rev. edition. London: A. C. Fifield, 1905.

Dolfin-Boldu, Contessa Norina. *Giornali di Carovana*. Milan: privately printed, 1934.

Douglas, Gertrude M. *Rifle Shooting for Ladies*. London: Arthur Pearson, 1910.

Douglas, Robert Dick, Jr., David R. Martin, Jr., and Douglas L. Oliver. *Three Boy Scouts in Africa On Safari with Martin Johnson*. New York: G. P. Putnam's Sons, 1928.

Dower, Lavender. *Epic Failure*. Edinburgh: William Blackwood & Sons, 1939.

Eastman, George. *Chronicles of an African Trip*. Rochester, NY: John P. Smith, 1927.

Eden, Frances (Fanny). *Tigers, Durbars and Kings: Fanny Eden's Indian Journals 1837–1838*, edited by Janet Dunbar. London: John Murray, 1988.

Fischer, Helen. *Peril Is My Companion*. London: Robert Hale, 1957.

Fleischmann, Max C. *After Big Game in Arctic and Tropic: A Sportsman's Note-Book of the Chase Off Greenland and Alaska; In Africa, Norway, Spitzbergen, and the Cassair*. Cincinnati: The Jennings and Graham Press, 1909.

Galton, Francis. *The Art of Travel; or, Shifts and Contrivances Available in Wild Countries (1872)*. Harrisburg: Stackpole Books, 1971.

Gardner, Mrs. Alan. *Rifle and Spear with the Rajpoots: Being the Narrative of a Winter's Travel and Sport in Northern India*. London: Chatto & Windus, 1895.

Grant, Claude H. B. *The Shikari: A Hunter's Guide*. Westminster, UK: The Research Publishing Co. Ltd., 1914.

Greville, The Lady, editor. *The Gentlewoman's Book of Sports*. London: Henry and Co., no date.

Gunn, Hugh. "The Sportsman as an Empire Builder." *Empire Big Game*. Edited by Hugh Gunn, 1–25. London: Simpkin, Marshall, Hamilton, Kent & Co., 1925.

——. *Ladies in the Field: Sketches of Sports*. New York: D. Appleton and Company, 1894.

Handley, Mrs. M. A. *Roughing It in Southern India*. London: Edward Arnold, 1911.

Harrell, Helen. *Safari. . . .* No place: privately printed, ca. 1952.

Harriman, E. Roland. *I Reminisce*. Garden City, NY: Doubleday, 1975.

Harriman, Gladys F. *A Journey of Adventure. Mexico, January, February 1938*. No place: privately printed, ca. 1938.

——. *B. C. in A. D. 1938*. No place: privately printed, ca. 1939.

——. *"Mulligan"*. No place: privately printed, ca. 1940.

Henderson, Kathleen C. T. *The Sporting Adventures of a Memsahib*. Madras: privately printed, 1918.

Herbert, Agnes. *Casuals in the Caucasus: The Diary of a Sporting Holiday*. London: John Lane, 1912.

——. *Two Dianas in Somaliland: The Record of a Shooting Trip*. London: John Lane, 1907.

Herbert, Agnes and A Shikári. *Two Dianas in Alaska*. London: John Lane, 1909.

Holmes, Bettie Fleischmann. *The Log of the "Laura" in Polar Seas: A Hunting Cruise from Tromsö, Norway to Spitsbergen, the Polar Ice off East Greenland and the Island of Jan Mayen in the Summer of 1906*. Cambridge, MA: The University Press, 1907.

Hubbard, Margaret. *African Gamble*. New York: G. P. Putnam's Sons, 1937.

Hunter, Rodello. *Wyoming Wife*. New York: Alfred A. Knopf, 1969.

Jenkins, Lady. *Sport & Travel in Both Tibets*. London: Blades, East & Blades, [1910].

Jessen, B. H. *W.N. McMillan's Expeditions and Big Game Hunting in the South Sudan, Abyssinia and East Africa*. London: Marchant Singer & Co., 1906.

Johnson, Clive W. *With Memsaab in the Arctic*. Los Angeles: privately printed, 1961.

——. *With Memsaab on Safari*. Los Angeles: privately printed, 1956.

——. *With Memsaab on the Rungwa*. Los Angeles: privately printed, 1958.

Johnson, Mrs. F. Kirk. *Safari Diary, 1961*. No place: privately printed, 1961.

Johnson, Martin. *Lion: African Adventures with the King of Beasts*. New York: G. P. Putnam's Sons, 1929.

Johnson, Osa. *Four Years in Paradise*. Garden City, NY: Garden City Publishing Co., Inc., 1941.

——. *I Married Adventure: The Lives and Adventures of Martin and Osa Johnson*. Philadelphia: J. B. Lippincott Company, 1940.

Kennedy, Bess. *The Lady and the Lions*. New York: Whittlesey House, McGraw Hill, 1942.

King, Mrs. E. L. *Hunting Big Game in Africa*. Winona, MN: privately printed, 1926.

Krag, Sonni. *Blandt Lover og Negrer i Afrikas Indre*. Oslo: Gyldenal Norsk Forlag, 1931.

Lane, Margaret. *Life with Ionides*. London: Hamish Hamilton, 1964.

Legendre, Gertrude Sanford. *The Time of My Life*. Charleston, SC: Wyrick & Co., 1987.

Littledale, St. George. "The Ovis Poli of the Pamir." In *Big Game Hunting*, vol. 2, *The Badminton Library of Sports and Pastimes*. Edited by Clive Phillipps-Wolley and the Duke of Beaufort. New ed. 363–376. London: Longmans, Green, and Co., 1903.

Lord, W. B., and T. Baines. *Shifts and Expedients of Camp Life, Travel & Exploration*. London: Horace Cox, 1871.

Lyell, Denis D. *Wild Life in Central Africa*. London: The Field & Queen, [1913].

MacDonald, Sheila. *Tanganyikan Safari*. Sydney: Angus & Robertson, 1948.

Madeira, Percy C. *Hunting in British East Africa*. Philadelphia: J. B. Lippincott Co., 1909.

Mallett, Marguerite. *A White Woman Among the Masai*. New York: E. P. Dutton, 1923.

Martelli, Mrs. C. "Tigers I Have Shot." In *Ladies in the Field. Sketches of Sport*. Edited by Lady Greville, 145–156. New York: D. Appleton, 1894.

Maturin, Mrs. Fred (Edith Cecil-Porch). *Adventures Beyond the Zambesi: Of the O'Flaherty; The Insular Miss; The Soldier Man, and the Rebel-Woman*. London: Eveleigh Nash, 1913.

McConnaughey, Lucille Harris. *Woman Afield*. New York: Vantage Press, 1987.

McCutcheon, John T. *In Africa. Hunting Adventures in the Big Game Country*. Indianapolis: Bobbs-Merrill Co., 1910.

Meikle, R. S., and Mrs. M. E. Meikle. *After Big Game: The Story of an African Holiday*. London: T. Werner Laurie Ltd., [1917].

Michael, Marjorie. *I Married a Hunter*. New York: G. P. Putnam's Sons, 1957.

Morden, Florence H. *From the Field Notebook of Florence H. Morden*. Concord, NH: The Rumford Press, 1940.

Morden, William and Irene. *Our African Adventure*. London: Seeley Service, 1954.

Morse, I. H., and Julie B. Morse. *Yankee in Africa*. Boston: The Stratford Company, 1936.

Morses, [The]. *Big Game Hunting in Africa and India*. Littleton, NH: privately printed, 1936.

Murray, Hilda. *Echoes of Sport*. London: T. N. Foulis, 1911.

Nané (Mrs. Tennant). *Safari. The Diary of a Novice: Big Game Hunting in Tanganyika*. No place: privately printed, 1937.

Ness, Mrs. Patrick. *Ten Thousand Miles in Two Continents*. London: Methuen & Co., Ltd., 1929.

Petherick, Mr. and Mrs. *Travels in Central Africa*. London: Tinsley Brothers, 1869.

Prescott, Marjorie Wiggin. *Tales of a Sportsman's Wife*. Boston: The Merrymount Press, 1936.

Radclyffe, C. R. E. *Big Game Shooting in Alaska*. London: Rowland Ward, Limited, 1904.

Ratclyffe, Dorothy Una. *Equatorial Dawn: Travel Letters from North, East, and Central Africa*. London: Eyre & Spottiswoode, 1936.

Roby, Marguerite. *My Adventures in the Congo*. London: Edward Arnold, 1911.

Roosevelt, Theodore. *African Game Trails: An Account of the African Wanderings of an American Hunter-Naturalist*. New York: Charles Scribner's Sons, 1910.

Savile, Frank. *The High Grass Trail. Being the Difficulties and Diversions of Two: Trekking, and Shooting for Sustenance in Dense Bush Across British Central Africa*. London: H. F. & G. Witherby, 1924.

Savory, Isabel. *A Sportswoman in India: Personal Adventures and Experiences of Travel in Known and Unknown India*. London: Hutchinson & Co., 1900.

Seton, Grace Gallatin. *Nimrod's Wife*. New York: Doubleday, Page & Company, 1907.

——. *"Yes, Lady Saheb": A Woman's Adventurings with Mysterious India*. New York: Harper & Brothers, 1925.

Seton, Grace Thompson. *Magic Waters: Through the Wild of Matto Grosso and Beyond*. New York: E. P. Dutton, 1933.

Seton-Karr, H. W. *Shores and Alps of Alaska*. London: Sampson Low, Marston, Searle, & Rivington, 1887.

Seton-Thompson, Grace Gallatin. *A Woman Tenderfoot*. New York: Doubleday, Page and Co., 1900.

Shaughnessy, Patrick and Diane Swingle. *Hard Hunting*. New York: Winchester Press, 1978.

Sheldon, Charles. *The Wilderness of the North Pacific Coast Islands*. New York: Charles Scribner's Sons, 1912.

Siemel, Sasha and Edith, and Gordon Schendel. *Jungle Wife*. Garden City, NY: Doubleday & Co., 1949.

Slaughter, Frances, editor. *Sportswoman's Library*. London: Archibald Constable, 1898.

Smythies, Olive. *Ten Thousand Miles on Elephants*. London: Seeley, Service & Co., 1961.

——. *Tiger Lady: Adventures in the Indian Jungle*. London: William Heinemann, 1953.

Speedy, Mrs. *My Wanderings in the Soudan*. London: Richard Bentley, 1884.

Sportsman, [The] (ed). *British Sports and Sportsmen. Big Game Hunting and Angling*. London: British Sports and Sportsmen, 1914.

St. Maur, Mrs. Algernon. *Impressions of a Tenderfoot, During a Journey in Search of Sport in the Far West*. London: John Murray, 1890.

Statham, Colonel J. C. B. *With My Wife Across Africa, By Canoe and Caravan*. London: Simpkin, Marshall, Hamilton, Kent & Co., Ltd., [1924].

Stewart, Elinor Pruitt. *Letters on an Elk Hunt by a Woman Homesteader*. Lincoln: University of Nebraska Press, 1979 (1915).

Strickland, Mrs. Diana. *Through the Belgian Congo*. London: Hurst & Blackett, 1924.

Sucksdorf, Astrid B. *Tiger in Sight*. New York: Delacorte Press, 1970.

Taylor, John. *African Rifles and Cartridges*. Georgetown, SC: Small Arms Technical Publishing Company, 1948.

Tyacke, Mrs. R. H. *How I Shot My Bears; or, Two Years' Tent Life in Kullu and Lahoul*. London: Sampson Low, Marston & Company, 1893.

Vanderbilt, Lucille Parsons. *Safari: Some fun! Some fun!* Sands Point, NY: privately printed, 1936.

Vassal, Gabrielle M. *Life in French Congo*. London: T. Fisher Unwin Ltd., 1925.

——. *On & Off Duty in Annam*. London: William Heinemann, 1910.

Warren, Donald and Lora. *Diary, Safari of 1956*. Los Angeles: privately printed, ca. 1957.

Wheatley, Harriet. *Lady Angler: Fishing, Hunting and Camping in Wilderness Areas of North America*. San Antonio: The Naylor Co., 1952.

Winans, Walter. *Shooting for Ladies*. New York: G. P. Putnam's Sons, 1911.

Younghusband, Ethel. *Glimpses of East Africa and Zanzibar*. London: John Long, 1910.

SECONDARY SOURCES

Adams, W. H. Davenport. *Celebrated Women Travellers of the Nineteenth Century*. London: W. Swan Sonnenschein, 1883.

Aiken, Maria. *A Girdle Around the Earth*. London: Constable, 1987.

Allen, Alexandra. *Travelling Ladies*. London: Jupiter, 1980.

Barnes, Frank C. *Cartridges of the World,* 3rd edition. Northfield, IL: Digest Books Inc., 1972.

Birkett, Dea. *Spinsters Abroad: Victorian Lady Explorers*. New York: Basil Blackwell, 1989.

Biscotti, M. L. *A Bibliography of American Sporting Books, 1926–1985*. Far Hills, NJ: Meadow Run Press Inc., 1997.

Brander, Michael. *The Big Game Hunters*. London: The Sportsman's Press, 1988.

Bull, Bartle. *Safari: A Chronicle of Adventure*. New York: Viking, 1988.

Cameron, Kenneth. *Into Africa: The Story of the East African Safari*. London: Constable, 1990.

Czech, Kenneth P. *An Annotated Bibliography of African Big Game Hunting Books, 1785–1950*. St. Cloud, MN: Land's Edge Press, 1999.

Delpar, Helen, editor. *The Discoverers: An Encyclopedia of Explorers and Exploration*. New York: McGraw-Hill, 1980.

Ferris, Elizabeth Fuller. "Preface." In Elinor Pruitt Stewart, *Letters on an Elk Hunt*. Lincoln: University of Nebraska Press, 1979.

Frawley, Maria H. *A Wider Range: Travel Writing by Women in Victorian England*. London: Associated University Presses, 1994.

Gassett, José Ortega y. *Meditations on Hunting*. Translated by Howard B. Wescott. New York: Charles Scribner's Sons, 1972.

Heller, Morris. *American Hunting and Fishing Books. An Annotated Bibliography of Books and Booklets on American Hunting and Fishing, 1900–1970*, Vol. 1. Mesilla, NM: Nimrod and Piscator Press, 1997.

Holman, Dennis. *Inside Safari Hunting with Eric Rundgren*. London: W. H. Allen, 1969.

Hoyem, George A. *The History and Development of Small Arms Ammunition, Vol. 3: British Sporting Rifle*. Tacoma: Armory Publications, 1985.

MacKenzie, John M. *The Empire of Nature: Hunting, Conservation and British Imperialism*. Manchester: Manchester University Press, 1988.

Mackenzie, John M. "Chivalry, Social Darwinism and Ritualised Killing: the Hunting Ethos in Central Africa up to 1914." In *Conservation in Africa; people, policies and practice*. Edited by David Anderson and Richard Grove, 41–61. Cambridge: Cambridge University Press, 1987.

——. "Hunting in Eastern and Central Africa in the Late Nineteenth Century, with Special Reference to Zimbabwe." In *Sport in Africa, Essays in Social History*. Edited by William J. Baker and James A. Mangan, 172–195. New York: Africana Publishing Co., 1987.

——. "The Imperial Pioneer and Hunter and the British Masculine Stereotype in Late Victorian and Edwardian Times." In *Manliness and Morality: Middle-Class Masculinity in Britain and America, 1800–1940*. Edited by J. A. Mangan and James Walvin, 176–198. New York: St. Martin's Press, 1987.

Middleton, Dorothy. *Victorian Lady Travellers*. New York: E. P. Dutton, 1965.

Miller, Luree. *On Top of the World: Five Women Explorers in Tibet*. Seattle: The Mountaineers, 1984.

Mills, Sarah. *Discourses of Difference: An Analysis of Women's Travel Writing and Colonialism*. London: Routledge, 1991.

Olds, Elizabeth Fagg. *Women of the Four Winds*. Boston: Houghton Mifflin, 1985.

Packenham, Thomas. *The Scramble for Africa, 1876–1912*. New York: Random House, 1991.

Phillips, John C. *A Bibliography of American Sporting Books*. New York: James Cummins Bookseller, 1991.

Roberts, Brian. *Ladies of the Veldt*. London: John Murray, 1965.

Robinson, Jane, editor. *Unsuitable for Ladies: An Anthology of Women Travellers*. Oxford: Oxford University Press, 1995.

Robinson, Jane. *Wayward Women: A Guide to Women Travellers*. Oxford: Oxford University Press, 1990.

Romero, Patricia W., editor. *Women's Voices on Africa: A Century of Travel Writings*. New York: Marcus Wiener Publishing, 1992.

Ruffer, Jonathan Garnier. *The Big Shots: Edwardian Shooting Parties*. New York: Debrett's Peerage Limited/The Viking Press, 1978.

Russell, Mary. *The Blessings of a Good Thick Skirt: Women Travellers and Their World*. London: Collins, 1986.

Shattock, Joanne. *The Oxford Guide to British Women Writers*. Oxford: Oxford University Press, 1993.

Stevenson, Catherine Barnes. *Victorian Women Travel Writers in Africa*. Boston: Twayne Publishers, 1982.

Stott, Kenhelm, Jr. *Exploring with Martin and Osa Johnson*. Chanute, KS: Martin and Osa Safari Museum Press, 1978.

Tiltman, Marjorie Hessell. *Women in Modern Adventure*. London: George G. Harrap & Co. Ltd., 1935.

Tinling, Marion. *Women into the Unknown: A Sourcebook on Women Explorers and Travelers*. Westport, CT: Greenwood, 1989.

Wheeler, Sessions S. *Gentleman in the Outdoors: A Portrait of Max C. Fleischmann*. Reno: University of Nevada Press, 1985.

Youngs, Tim. *Travellers in Africa: British Travelogues, 1850–1900*. Manchester: Manchester University Press, 1994.

ARTICLES, UNPUBLISHED THESES, AND PAPERS

Bassett, Troy. "A Dangerous Woman: The Representation of Big-Game Hunter Lady Jenkins in Antonia William's *Recollections of Somaliland, 1904–1905*." Paper presented at Writing the Journey: A Conference on American, British and Anglophone Travel Writers and Writing, Philadelphia, June 10–13,1999.

Bennett, Scott. "Shikar and the Raj." *South Asia*, vol. 7 (1984): 72–88.

Birkett, Dea and Julie Wheelwright. " 'How Could She?' Unpalatable Facts and Feminists' Heroines." *Gender & History*, vol. 2 (1990): 49–57.

Blaikie, W. G. "Lady Travellers." *Blackwood's Magazine*, vol. 160 (1896): 49–66.

Czech, Kenneth. "With Rifle and Petticoat: Agnes Herbert, a British Woman in the Haunts of Big Game." Paper presented at the Thirty-Fourth Annual Northern Great Plains History Conference, St. Cloud, MN, October 7–9, 1999.

Franey, Laura. "Violent Equality: A Reappraisal of Travel and Fin-de-Siecle Feminism." Paper presented at Snapshots From Abroad: A Conference on American and British Travel Writers and Writing, Minneapolis, Nov. 14–16, 1997.

Petherick, Katherine. "Mrs. Petherick's African Journal." *Blackwood's Magazine*, vol. 91 (1862): 673–701.

Roe, Kathy Juanita. *Five Victorian Women Explorers in Africa, 1856–1900.* Master's thesis, Winthrop College, 1976.

Sramek, Joseph. "An English Lady in the French Colonies: Gabrielle Vassal and Her Travelogues on Vietnam, Southern China and the French Congo." *Suite 101.com* (Nov. 2000). <http://www.suite101.com/article.cfm/945/30959>.

NEWSPAPER AND PERIODICALS

Academy
Atheneum
Birmingham Post
Book
Booklist
Bookman
Boston Transcript
Chicago Daily Tribune
Dial
Library Journal
Minneapolis Star Tribune
Nation
New Republic
New Statesman
New York Herald
New York Times
Outlook
Saturday Review of Literature
Spectator
Springfield Republican
The Times (London) Literary Supplement
Winona (MN) Sunday News

Index